CISTERCIAN FATHERS SERIES : NUMBER THIRTY-SEVEN

BERNARD OF CLAIRVAUX

Volume Thirteen

FIVE BOOKS ON CONSIDERATION

Advice to a Pope

THE WORKS OF BERNARD OF CLAIRVAUX

Volume Thirteen

Five Books On

ADVICE TO A POPE

Original title:

De consideratione ad Eugenium papam tertiam libri quinque

CISTERCIAN FATHERS SERIES : NUMBER THIRTY-SEVEN

Consideration

translated by JOHN D. ANDERSON & ELIZABETH T. KENNAN

CISTERCIAN PUBLICATIONS

A Cistercian Publications title published by Liturgical Press

Cistercian Publications
Editorial Offices
161 Grosvenor Street
Athens, Ohio 45701
www.cistercianpublications.org

The translation here presented is based on the critical Latin edition
prepared by Jean Leclercq and Henri Rochais under the sponsorship of the
S. Order of Cistercians and published by Editiones Cistercienses,
Piazza Tempio di Diana, 14
I-00153 Rome, Italy.

*The work of Cistercian Publications is made possible in part by support
from Western Michigan University to the Institute of Cistercian Studies.*

Book design by GALE AKINS
Cover design by ELIZABETH KING
Typeset at HUMBLE HILLS PRESS

Library of Congress Catalogue Card Number: 75-27953
ISBN (paperback) 978-0-87907-737-2

CONTENTS

Introduction by Elizabeth T. Kennan   3

St Bernard's Five Books on Consideration: Advice to a Pope
   Preface   23
   Book One   25
   Book Two   47
   Book Three   79
   Book Four   109
   Book Five   139

Appendices by Bernard Jacqueline
   The Recipient   183
   Date of Composition   184
   Manuscripts   184
   Sources   185
   Influence   187
   Plan   189

Notes   193

Selected Bibliography   211

Analytic Index   217

Index of Proper Names   220

ABBREVIATIONS

Biblical sources are cited according to the abbreviations of the Revised Standard Version. Psalm references are made according to the Vulgate enumeration.

Mansi, *Concil.* = J. D. Mansi, *Sacrorum conciliorum nova et amplissima collectio,* 31 vols. Florence-Venice, 1759-98. Rpt. Graz: Akademische Druck- und Verlagsanstalt. 1960.

With filial homage

the Editors of

Cistercian Publications

dedicate this volume

to the present successor of Blessed Eugene III

PAUL VI

FIVE BOOKS ON CONSIDERATION
ADVICE TO A POPE

INTRODUCTION

I

INTRODUCTION

SAINT BERNARD was born in 1090 to a prolific but fairly minor Burgundian family. Inherited properties centered at Fontaine-les-Dijon supported knightly professions for most of his immediate relatives and permitted some largesse to local ecclesiastical institutions. Bernard's mother, Aleth, was one of those women remarkable in any age: pious, fiercely strong, capable of eliciting passionate affection from her children. Of them all, Bernard received her most concentrated attention and his formation in the spiritual life is attributed by contemporary biographers to her. As a younger son and a delicate boy, he was not trained for farming and fighting, but sent nearby for a clerical education. There is no record of Bernard's school-time training, but it fixed an exquisite classical calque to his written style that remained throughout his life. He seldom quotes a pagan author, and yet, the aesthetic sense of balance and rhythm in his language and the rhetorical structure of his arguments are unquestionably classical.

Bernard's spiritual growth in adolescence is almost as unknown to us as his academic formation. The *Vita Prima* reports an early and strong sense of purity and retells of a series of salacious temptations which might have put the virtue of a weaker youth to the test. More important, it indicates in him a natural tendency to compunction, that

3

combination of self knowledge and sense of sin which is the keystone of monastic spiritual life. Whatever else, Bernard must have had an almost fierce rigorousness about him, for when he made his option for monastic life at twenty two, amidst all the grandeur of monasticism in Burgundy, he chose the tiny, strict, and almost starving community of Cîteaux.

Bernard was only to be a simple monk for three years. In 1115, after a year's novitiate and two years professed life, he was sent as abbot to found Cîteaux's third daughter house at Clairvaux. There, for the remainder of his life, he was engaged in the spiritual formation of those who, by the hundreds, flocked to his tutelage. His is one of the most impressive abbacies in the history of the church. Not only did Clairvaux attract a spectacular recruitment during his lifetime, it founded or affiliated seventy daughter houses which, in turn, engendered ninety-four more. By 1153, Clairvaux alone was responsible for as many dependent monasteries as Cîteaux and its other three major daughter houses combined. The monastic network headed by Clairvaux spread throughout Europe. It was paralleled by another network of ecclesiastical officials ranging from bishops to a pope, who were trained as monks in Bernard's monastery.

Despite his larger role in ecclesiastical politics, Bernard's first responsibility was to teach and discipline these men, and he fulfilled it. He visited the novices regularly, and not only preached to the monks but kept a close eye on their demeanor. With men of unusual intellectual gifts or spiritual delicacy such as Henry Murdac, Guerric of Igny or William of Saint Thierry, Bernard became a confidant. For the monks in Clairvaux's daughter houses, to whom he owed a debt of guidance but whom he could not visit, he wrote a remarkable series of sermons, designed for study, so that he could enter their meditation and direct it. Monks who left Clairvaux for other ecclesiastical responsibilities took Bernard's continuing solicitude with them. As abbot of Fountains, Henry Murdac was counselled and reprimanded by Bernard, who still considered himself a spiritual father to the other abbot. As pope, the former monk of Clairvaux, Eugene III, received repeated advice from his abbot of which the *De consideratione* is the culmination.

Bernard's political activity was intimately connected to his vocation and never supplanted it. He was born just five years after the death of the intrepid reforming pope, Gregory VII, and was raised in Burgundy, the heartland of reform monasticism. The community he entered in 1112, Cîteaux, was at the vanguard of that pure primitivism which was so characteristic of the second generation of reformers. In Bernard's first years as abbot, his closest associate was the impeccable William of Champeaux, Bishop of Chalons-sur-Marne, one of the earliest scholastics and founder of the pioneering Augustinian Abbey of St. Victor in Paris.

Bernard's reform credentials were unimpeachable. When papal schism in 1130 created a sharp and shocking political rift in the church, Bernard spoke eloquently for the party which he considered to represent the authentic reform tradition. And he spoke to great effect. In the summer following the disputed election, he attended a council of the French church at Etampes convoked by Louis VI to determine the legitimate pope. Bernard's passionate endorsement of Innocent II was a major factor in the French decision to recognize him and reject the claims of his rival, Anacletus II.

The next year, Bernard catapulted from papal advocate to advisor. Travelling through France, the exiled Innocent II gathered Bernard into his party and brought him for the first time into an intimacy with reigning popes which was to last for the remainder of his life. He became Innocent's chief representative: his intercession brought

Henry I of England into the reform camp and won the
support of Germany. When the Duke of Aquitaine
reneged after first acquiescing to Bernard's candidate, he
terrified him into subservience. On the reentry of Innocent
to Italy, it was Bernard who was sent to bring Milan, Pisa
and Genoa to their knees. At the end, when Roger of
Sicily pretended that a successful public debate would
dislodge him from support of the Anacletan party, Bernard
was Innocent's debater. Thus, Innocent's victory in Rome
in 1138 brought to Bernard vast political capital which was
to last not only for the remainder of that papacy but
throughout the line of popes established by Innocent,
reaching its climax at the elevation of his own pupil,
Eugene III.

Throughout this period until his death in 1153, Bernard
acted as unofficial and sometimes as unsolicited counsel
to the popes. He undertook broadly diverse missions at
their behest: in 1135, for example, he was sent to Bamberg to reconcile Frederick of Hohenstaufen to Lothar III,
the newly minted Emperor of the Romans; ten years later
he was sent to the Midi to reconcile the Cathars to
orthodoxy. At Eugene's behest he preached the Second
Crusade. But he also entered as party to actions on his own
initiative, seeking to move the Curia to his point of view.
The most famous of these instances occurred at the Council of Rheims in 1148 where, by concerted lobbying, he
attempted to force condemnation of Gilbert of Poitiers.
By more regular channels, he nudged the popes to use
their appellate jurisdiction to uphold the cause of reform
at Langres and at York. In all these matters he brought to
bear his unique experience as contemplative, as abbot, as
mystic and as politician, to the problems of the reform
church.

These were the problems of success. Between 1130 and
1153 the great victories of the first reform period were
consolidated. Outside Sicily there was, for the moment,

no serious opposition to reform politics. Germany, which had so disrupted the first two generations of reform, was strangely subdued. In the succession crisis which followed the extinction of the direct Salian line· in 1125, the great ecclesiastics had a clear advantage over other aristocratic factions by virtue of their cohesion and set purpose. They had already won significant concessions three years earlier when the Concordat of Worms recognized the principle of ecclesiastical election. The Archbishop of Mainz pressed home that advantage, forcing the new king, Lothar of Supplinburg, whose election he had personally secured, to abrogate his rights to be present at elections and to demand homage from ecclesiastics. Papal schism in 1130, which ten years before would have presented tempting possibilities to raid the church and humiliate the pope, brought little advantage to Lothar III. So indebted was he to the party of ecclesiastical reform in Germany that it took no more than a single visit from Saint Bernard to bring him irrevocably into the Innocent's camp. His successor in 1138, Conrad of Hohenstaufen, was little better placed. Brought to the throne by the maneuvering of Adalbero, Bishop of Trier, Conrad's political future depended on the continued support of the reformers. Not until Frederick Barbarossa consolidated the purely aristo-cratic factions in 1152 could the German king afford to challenge the great ecclesiastics. In the interim, Lothar and Conrad momentarily approached that role of sword-bearer to Saint Peter which was to become so central a tenet of papal faith in the later middle ages.

In fact, the victory of the reform party in Italy depended on German military support. In 1133, Lothar mounted an expedition, puny enough in itself, to bring Innocent south as far as the Lateran palace. Although he did not have force enough to dislodge the Anacletans from the basilica of Saint Peter, Innocent rewarded him with imperial coronation at the church of Saint John Lateran. In the accompanying negotiations, the pope secured confirmation of German ecclesiastical liberties and even won recognition of his suzerainty over the Mathildine lands of Tuscany, long disputed with the Salian dynasty. Papal influence in Germany, the trigger for these concessions, was demonstrated again in the following year when Lothar returned home to discover that his Hohenstaufen enemies had raided his local bases. When the ecclesiastical party, led by Bernard of Clairvaux as papal envoy, brought them to task at Bamberg in 1135, Lothar repaid this intervention with another army for Italy, large enough to establish the Innocentians in many northern cities and to attack the Anacletan party in its particular stronghold, the southern domains of Roger of Sicily. After Lothar died in December 1137, Conrad III managed to avoid any further Italian expeditions. But against all calculation of secular advantage, he succumbed to Saint Bernard's appeals for military service in the papal cause by leading a precipitously mounted army to extinction in the Second Crusade.

Close relations with Germany after fifty years of war had important consequences for the papacy. The vast German church with its populous Rhineland dioceses and its important vantage for missions to the East was at last brought into the sphere of papal influence. Free ecclesiastical elections elevated bishops sympathetic to the papacy in dioceses that were developing vigorously. Papal legates, now able to travel widely in German territories and intervene in diocesan affairs, brought occasional outside supervision to ecclesiastical courts. Grants of exemption to German monasteries made the papacy a court of first instance in adjudicating many claims to monastic property. At the same time, Cistercian houses spreading into the Rhineland and beyond gave a popular and moral dimension to the papal presence which might otherwise have been purely administrative.

In France and England, too, there was a vigorous expansion of papal influence between 1130 and 1153. Louis VI of France, constantly harrassed by feudal brigands, was willing to accept papal reinforcement to his prestige and to support the Innocentine party in the broad aspects of policy. Although never willing to submit to papal demands for full freedom of ecclesiastical elections, he nonetheless allowed—or was powerless to stop—communication between French churchmen and the Curia. His son, Louis VII, was more closely aligned with Rome. Overcome by remorse after cremating the villagers of Vitry in their own church in 1143, Louis submitted himself to the personal guidance of Eugene and of Bernard. Out of that submission came the Second Crusade, and papal influence in France peaked in the winter of 1145–46 when Bernard preached the crusade, everywhere taking papal indulgence and papal authority to the faithful.

Although the crusade was not preached in England with the same vigor as it was on the continent, nonetheless, here too it inspired an expedition. More significant for papal power in England, however, was the succession crisis which followed the death of Henry I in 1135. Henry's last-minute heir, Stephen of Blois, faced a serious challenge from his cousin, Henry's daughter Mathilda. Like Lothar in Germany, he depended on the great ecclesiastics and especially upon his brother, Henry, Bishop of Winchester, to shore up his claims. Hardly a reformer of the Cistercian cast (Bernard called him the whore of Babylon), Henry of Winchester had important ties to Rome through the old Burgundian party. It was he who brought papal influence to dead center in English politics. After his consecration by the Archbishop of Canterbury in 1135, Stephen immediately announced his confirmation by Pope Innocent. He issued a sweeping charter of liberties for the English church which fully acquiesced to the gains of the Gregorian papacy. Despite

his initial anxiety to please the great churchmen, however,
Stephen forfeited their confidence, along with that of
most of the political class, in the course of four years'
misrule. Mathilda's invasion of 1139 led to civil war and
then anarchy. In the subsequent confusion, Henry of Winchester, now papal legate for England, swung the official
church into the balance by calling two legatine councils in
quick succession, one in April 1141 to pronounce for
Mathilda and another in December to restore Stephen.

Ecclesiastical action alone was not decisive in 1141 and
Henry's own influence waned after loss of his legatine
status in 1143, but the English church gained enormous
political freedom during the anarchy. Its ties with con-
tinental reformers and with Rome in particular were greatly
strengthened. The Cistercians drove a wide wedge in
English monastic life. Their houses increased from five in
1135 to 27 in 1147, and most of these were filiated to
Clairvaux. It was Cistercian insistence on enforcing the
newest reform decrees which created a disputed election at
York in 1141, cutting across the entire political matrix of
the North, and inviting repeated papal interventions.

Papal gains along the Mediterranean were by no means
as dramatic as this. On the Iberian peninsula, recognition
by a papal legate made the Count of Portugal a king in
1143. And legates in Castile and Aragon seem to have
taken a regular place at the head of the Spanish church,
convoking synods at Valladolid and Gerona, and personally realigning the network of diocesan boundaries.
But in Italy, the wayward development of the central and
northern cities, including Rome, made papal leadership
singularly ineffective. Rome itself in 1143 rebelled against
papal temporal power, revived the ancient Senate, and
declared itself a republic. It was to remain in rebellion well
beyond the death of Eugene III. Pope Lucius III was
killed in action against the republicans in 1145 when he
led an army to storm the Capitol. Eugene fled the city

only three days after his election when an armed mob prevented his entry to St. Peter's for consecration. In 1148 he too would lead an army to gain a foothold for himself at Rome.

Part of the papal weakness at Rome stemmed from the rupture of its relations—tenuous as they were—with the Sicilian Normans. In 1139 at Mignano, Innocent II had entered into an enforced peace with Roger of Sicily, but neither he nor his successors made the least headway in bringing the principles of reform to that kingdom. Lucius III, for reasons that are not clear, broke off all contact with Roger and left himself and his successors without a local ally in struggles against the commune.

In spite of the Italian situation, however, the papal party by 1153 had reason to congratulate itself on its political victories. In Germany, England, France, Portugal, Aragon and Castile, for the moment at least, local churches were firmly aligned with the Roman hierarchy. Only Roger of Sicily among western monarchs could prevent penetration of his realm by papal agents or close communication between local churchmen and the Curia. Although the dramatic failure of the Second Crusade struck at the pope's spiritual leadership, the growth of Cistercian monasticism everywhere reinforced faith in the righteousness of the reform papacy. At mid-century, then, the pope had both the political and the moral advantages necessary to build an international government. To do so, he needed only administrative genius and the clairvoyance to prevent administration from choking charisma.

It is to these two requirements that the *De consideratione* is addressed. Better than any of his contemporaries, Saint Bernard grasped the complex play of attitudes which made papal leadership tolerated and even sought. He believed passionately in the assertion of that leadership, necessary to bring a chastened people to the Lord. He appreciated that outside the cloister the examples of saintliness alone could not accomplish this end. But he also knew that without saintliness, manipulation and power were equally useless. And so, he ruminated on the interplay of all three in what became a complex treatise on spiritual government.

The work is divided into five major sections, designated books. Each of the first four books treats a major aspect of papal office and policy. The fifth, the longest by far, touches the theological problems of knowing God and speculates as to the nature of the heavenly hierarchy.

Despite the celestial finale of the *De consideratione,* Book One begins prosaically enough. In it Bernard scrutinizes the papal calendar and exposes a disastrously overloaded schedule. The pressure of hearing litigation in particular, he argues, has submerged all other functions of the office. This abuse must be corrected before any others for it both distorts the office and cripples the man who holds it. To provide a motive for pruning routine obligations and to recall Eugene to the essence of his spiritual commitment, Bernard discusses the necessity of leisure within the confines of responsibility. Leisure is the source both of vitality and of wisdom, for it provides the opportunity to consider oneself and to conceive righteous decisions in regard to the business at hand. Consideration in this context focuses on defining virtue, and Bernard recalls the objects of such reasoning to Eugene toward the end of the book in an extended passage on the inter-relation of the four cardinal virtues. His argument concludes with the obvious but often disregarded caveat that such leisured consideration cannot be total. The pope's calendar must be reduced but it can hardly be expunged, nor can it even be freed totally of minor business. Even temporal disputes may occasionally have spiritual consequences which force the pope to attend them. But, though litigation will go on, the procedures used in the papal court can be so streamlined as to eliminate wrangling and enforce honesty by clear and brief argumentation.

Saint Bernard urged consideration as a practical measure, a prudent prelude to action, in Book One. By
contrast, he opens the next book with retrospective
consideration of a completed act which contemporaries
damned as unconsidered and rash: the initiation of the
Second Crusade. Bernard and Eugene shared the blame for
the catastrophic outcome of this expedition, and Bernard
recognized that its failure called into question the authen-
ticity of their spiritual commission. But to this he could
not speak, for he had acted simply at papal behest in
preaching the crusade. He could only offer some explanation for God's wrath in the waywardness of the troops and
the trials imposed by God upon the Israelites of old.

Once this matter is cleared away, Bernard moves to a
more complete definition of consideration. As opposed to
contemplation, which deals with truths already known,
consideration seeks truth in contingent human affairs
where it is difficult to perceive. In papal affairs, consideration investigates four separate spheres: the pope himself,
his subjects, his surroundings and the celestial hierarchy
above him which provides a model for the rest.

After this general introduction to the problems of papal
consideration, the remainder of the book is directed to
Eugene's own person. Knowledge of self is a complex
problem for a pope. It involves first of all a knowledge of
the man in office and, therefore, definition of that office.
In this context, Bernard insists that the pontificate is no
more than a ministry and in bold terms contrasts
ecclesiastical stewardship with secular dominion. The
pope is not a sovereign and the quality of his charge is
stewardship not rule. But this is not to say that his charge
to care for the church is anything less than absolute.
Among bishops the pope is prince, and over the hierarchy
he has a plenitude of power that allows him to correct, to
quash and to translate without reference to any other

body. Such is the implication of Peter's commission.

Knowledge of the pope's role in the church, however, is not the end of his self-consideration. Eugene must also know himself as a man, as a sinner and as a lover of the Lord. With a poignant exposition of the human state and a brief reminder of the inherent unity of all the virtues, Bernard closes Book Two.

Book Three examines the state of the church subjected to papal rule. It provides a brilliant survey of the abuses prevalent at mid-century after a long period of expansion: ambition and avarice among ecclesiastical officials, misuse of appeals to the curia, disruption of the hierarchy by intemperate granting of exemptions and failure by bishops and pope alike to enforce conciliar legislation. It is Bernard's most direct call for reform root and branch.

Bernard moves on in the next book to consider Eugene's surroundings, the City, the curia and the household. The discussion is set in revolutionary Rome which in the 1140's had twice driven popes from its boundaries and which in the 1150's was still in a state of armed insurrection. As the pope's immediate diocese as well as the seat of his government and chief shrine for pilgrimages in the West, Rome in rebellion presented agonizing problems for Eugene. Bernard investigates for him the alternative means of dealing with the crisis. He is clear that Eugene must take action, but rejects any direct military offensive. To make his point, he develops the famous image of the two swords (one symbolizing spiritual, the other temporal power) which became so integral a part of political thought in the subsequent century. It is the spiritual sword which the pope must apply; he must preach to his people even after they have taken to the streets. If they remain in arms, then let them be excommunicated. But if this sanction should fail, then without military support from the emperor, the pope can only flee the city.

The discussion of the curia which follows is an intriguing

indication of Bernard's preferred solution to the problem of reform. Well aware of abuses among the pope's servants, he offers no institutional remedies. Instead, with disarming directness, he simply prescribes: improve your personnel. With the wry observation that Rome can more easily find good men than make them, Bernard outlines in great detail the tests for employing suitable ministers. He is sanguine about their careers; once papal business is entrusted to men who are trustworthy, then *ipso facto* the failures of the system will disappear. The same is true for the papal household. A strict sense of priorities, close discipline and faith in a competent, honest staff will solve the domestic issue, leaving the pope free to be what he must be, the Vicar of Christ.

Thus far Bernard's consideration has been directed to practical affairs. The treatise presupposes but does not discuss the ultimate springs of ecclesiastical action. Book Five corrects this imbalance. In it Bernard directs consideration to God and explores the modes of comprehending the faith. He speculates on the nature of the celestial hierarchy, so crucial as a model for the hierarchy below. His discourse then soars to God, understood as principle of Being, as Trinity and as perfect unity. Finally, in a characteristically Bernardine manner, God is presented under four human aspects of comprehension: length, breadth, height and depth. Under these categories men can perceive divine eternity, charity, majesty and wisdom. More importantly, the categories themselves can elicit a psychological reaction in the beholder, inspiring in him both the fear and the humility which prepare for salvation.

Despite the clear principles on which the *De consideratione* is organized, it is a very difficult work. Written for two distinct ends, it is both a treatise on the politics of theocracy and a paternal admonition to a spiritual son whose very soul is imperiled by his office. Bernard wrote

as an abbot, he also wrote as a political strategist, and in
this treatise he inextricably mixed the two modes of
thought.

In undertaking to advise Eugene, Bernard addressed a
man existing at the center of an unbearable paradox. The
pope was at the same time a Cistercian monk and the
most harried administrator in western Christendom.
The tension between his two roles was irreducible. As a
Cistercian, Eugene was dedicated to the perfection of his
own spiritual life. His being was centered in prayer, in
study and in contemplation of God. But as pope, Eugene
was responsible for the administration of the Curia, the
regulation of the hierarchy, the protection of monasteries,
the safety of the Holy Land, the morality of the powerful,
the health and well being of the widowed and orphaned
and, not least, the reconquest of Rome. That work load
made the New Jerusalem look like a mirage.

For Eugene, the conflict between spirituality and
responsibility was pitched to extraordinary height, because
of the exacting standards of his spiritual commitment as a
Cistercian. But the paradox exists for every pope. Absolute standards of right conduct applicable to the cloister
where the monastic vow demands them and simplicity of
life permits them are simply not applicable to the
papacy. Here the demands of business and the weight of
power distract and deflect spiritual responsibility. Paradox
is at the very heart of spiritual government.

It is Bernard's genius to have cast the *De consideratione*
largely in terms of this paradox. Every major choice for
Eugene is cast in the form of an antithesis, dramatizing
the conflicts of his situation. But instead of urging one set
of alternatives on the pope as a matter of policy, Bernard
tries to preserve the tension between opposites and ex-
pose a middle course between them, thus honoring the
inherent paradox of the situation. What is more, this strict
adherence to the median way allows Bernard to develop

the classical rule of virtue: moderation in all things. This, in turn, becomes the touchstone of reform for him.

In strong contrast to Arnold of Brescia and other root and branch reformers, Bernard always remained a pragmatist. He had a clear perception that the possibilities for moral acts are circumscribed by fact. Where the Arnoldists condemned all ecclesiastical wealth and power and made of apostolic poverty the shibboleth of reform, Bernard remained flexible. He knew, and he took pains to point out, that power and wealth were no part of the Petrine inheritance. But he counselled that where a pope had gold and silver he might use them to meet the needs of the day. Money in itself was not an evil but only the attitude of men who loved it.

Likewise, adherance to the mean provided his standard for reforming the papal court. Despite its apparent pettifogging, the tenacious record-keeping and general disinterestedness of the papal curia had, by 1148, made it the most popular appellate court in Europe. No one at Rome was prepared to deal with the cases which flooded in on appeal by mid-century. A conscientious pontiff like Eugene might try to judge them all by himself, risking stupefation in the sheer press of litigation. The alternative process of delegating cases was still haphazard. Delays in obtaining a hearing were often long and problems of precedence and procedure gave opportunity to venality. And, round the confusion of the court, lawyers clustered like wasps on a fig tree, giving an impression of self seeking that threatened to undermine the very confidence that had distinguished the curia.

In discussing these problems, Bernard cast his observations in a series of antitheses. The very concept of the pope as judge had its paradoxical elements for him since Paul had advised Christians to "set them to judge who are most despised in the Church." If this precept were to be followed, papal justice might be abolished entirely. But

Bernard could no more countenance that than its opposite, permitting the current chaos of court practice to continue. Instead he prescribed a middle course: reduce the case load, accept no secular appeals unless there are clear spiritual issues involved, establish other judges with power to decide matters with full papal authority and, above all, excise the pernicious influence of the lawyers.

The *De consideratione* is surprising in its practicality. Its language is so intense and its rhetorical play on antithesis so dramatic that a reader is seldom prepared for the cool hardheadedness of Bernard's final proposals. And yet, this is perhaps after all not so surprising in a man who spent his lifetime as the head of one of history's most successful communities of men.

Elizabeth T. Kennan

The Catholic University of America
Washington, D.C.

EDITOR'S NOTE

The translation presented here is based on the edition of the *De consideratione ad Eugenium Papam* prepared by Jean Leclercq and Henri Rochais and published by Editiones Cistercienses in Rome in 1963 in volume three of the *S. Bernardi opera* (pp. 393–493). In the translation we have retained the section (Roman) and paragraph (Arabic) numbers and the subtitles found in this critical edition. These subtitles are not found in the majority of the twelfth-century manuscripts, but they are common after that time (see the Introduction to the edition, p. 391). We should like to thank Msgr. Bernard Jacquelin for his kindness in preparing the informative notes to be found in the Appendices, as well as the translators, Dr. John D. Anderson and Professor Elizabeth Kennan. We are especially grateful to Professor Kennan for having taken time out from her important work as Director of the Medieval and Byzantine Studies Program at The Catholic University of America to write the Introduction for this new translation.

M.B.P.

FIVE BOOKS ON CONSIDERATION
ADVICE TO A POPE

TEXT

PREFACE

I T HAS OCCURRED TO ME to write something which might edify, delight or console you, Blessed Father Eugene. But I do not know the rules for writing a formal yet intimate treatise. Two opposites, your majesty and my love, vie to dictate my style. Love draws me on; majesty holds me back. But you graciously intervene and request rather than command this treatise, although it would be more fitting for you to command it. Since your majesty so admirably condescends, why does my hesitancy persist? What if you have ascended the throne? Even if you were to walk on the wings of the wind,* you would not escape my affection. Love knows no master. It recognizes a son even though he wear the tiara[1]. It is the nature of a lover to be suitably humble, willingly submissive, freely compliant, respectful without duress. This is not the way with others however; they are driven either by fear or by greed. Such men bless openly, but harbor evil in their hearts.* They flatter you when you are present, yet fail

*Ps 103:3

*Ps 27:3

23

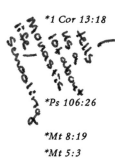

Monastic life is talked about & tells us of

*1 Cor 13:18

*Ps 106:26

*Mt 8:19

*Mt 5:3

*Job 29:16

you in time of need. But charity never fails.* It is true that I have been freed of maternal obligation toward you, but I am not stripped of affection for you. You were once in my womb; you will not be drawn from my heart so easily. Ascend to the heavens, descend to the depths,* you will not escape me. I shall follow you wherever you go.* I loved you when you were poor in spirit;* I shall love you still as father of the poor and the rich. If I know you, you did not cease being poor in spirit when you became the father of the poor.* I am confident that this change has been thrust upon you and was not of your doing, that this promotion has not replaced your former state, but rather has enhanced it. Therefore, I will instruct you not as a teacher, but as a mother, indeed, as a lover. I may seem more the fool[2], but only to one who does not love, to one who does not feel the force of love[3].

BOOK ONE

AN INQUIRY ABOUT THE DEMANDS
OF HIS OFFICE

NOW WHERE SHALL I BEGIN?
I would like to start with the
demands of your office, because I
especially share your grief over them. I
should say, 'share your grief,' however,
only if you are in fact grieving. Otherwise,
I should rather have said, 'I grieve,' because
you cannot share grief if no one else is
grieving. Therefore, if you grieve, I share
your grief; if you do not, I still grieve, and
very much so, knowing that a limb that is
numb draws farther from health and a sick
man who is unaware of his condition is in
greater danger.[1] Far be it from me, however, to suspect you of this. I am aware of
the pleasant delights of solitude you enjoyed not long ago. You cannot have
become unaccustomed to them this quickly.
You cannot so suddenly cease to grieve for
them: they were only recently taken from
you. A fresh wound cannot fail to cause
grief. Your wound has not yet begun to
heal; in so short a time its pain has not
ceased. Furthermore, unless you deceive
yourself, there is continual cause for

25

legitimate grief from daily injuries. Unless I am wrong, you are taken from the embrace of your Rachel against your will,* and as many times as you experience this suffering, your grief will necessarily be renewed.[2] But when do you not experience it? How often do you desire her, but in vain? How often do you move, but not advance? How often do you try, but achieve nothing? How often do you labor, but not give birth? How often do you strive, only to be interrupted? You fail even as you begin; just as you start, they cut you off. 'The sons came to the moment of birth,' says the Prophet, 'but she has no strength to bear them.'* Do you recognize this situation? Surely you do. If you are at peace when your affairs have so encroached upon you, you have become hardened like the heifer Ephraim, who was taught to love threshing.* I hope this is not the case with you, for this is the lot of a man who has been left to his own depravity.* It is a peace free of these affairs, not a peace with them, that I desire for you. There is nothing on your behalf that I fear more than that kind of peace. Do you wonder if it can ever happen? It can indeed, if, as is usual, a problem comes to be neglected through force of habit. *(as noted in intro, believes in retaining the paradox)*

*Gen 29:6 ff.

*4 Kings 19:3

*Hos 10:11

*Rom 1:28

THE DANGERS OF BEING OVERBURDENED

II. 2. Do not trust too much in your present dispositions. Nothing is so fixed in the soul as not to decay with neglect and time. A scab forms over an old, neglected sore, and as it becomes insensible, it becomes incurable. Indeed, a constant sharp pain cannot be borne for a long time. If it is not relieved by something external, it must provide its own relief. It is a fact that it will either obtain relief quickly from a cure or produce numbness by its own persistence. Is there anything that habit cannot pervert? Anything that is not dulled by frequent occurrence? Anything that is not overcome by repetition? How often do men dread something disagreeable which later becomes agreeable through habit? Hear how the Just Man laments about this: 'That which my soul would not touch before, now in my anguish has become my food.'* At first something will seem unbearable, but as time goes on, if you get used to it, you will think it is not so bad. A little later it will seem easy. Later still you will not notice it, and finally it will delight you. Thus you descend to hardness of heart and from there to apostasy.[3] It is as I said before: a continually severe pain will end quickly either by a cure or by numbness.

in general, addressing the problem of complacency

*Job 6:7

3. This is precisely why I have continually feared for you. And I fear now that you have delayed the remedy and, not able to bear the pain, you are plunging into danger in utter despair. I am afraid that you will despair of an end to the many demands that are made upon you and become calloused and gradually suppress your sense of just and useful pain. It would be much wiser to remove yourself from these demands even for a while, than to

allow yourself to be distracted by them and led, little by little, where you certainly do not want to go. Where? To a hard heart. Do not go on to ask what that is; if you have not been terrified by it, it is yours already. A hard heart is precisely one which does not shudder at itself because it is insensitive. But why ask me? Ask Pharoah.* No one with a hard heart has ever attained salvation, as the Prophet says, unless God in his mercy has taken from him a heart of stone and given him a heart of flesh.* Now, what is a hard heart? One that is not torn by compunction,[4] softened by piety, or moved by entreaty. It does not yield to threats; it becomes obdurate with beatings. It is ungrateful for kindness, treacherous in its advice, harsh in judgment, unashamed of disgrace, fearless in danger, inhuman toward humanity, brazen toward divinity, unmindful of the past, neglectful of the present, improvident toward the future. This is a heart which recalls nothing at all from the past except injuries suffered, retains nothing of the present and makes neither provision nor preparation for the future except perhaps in vengeance. To encompass all the evils of such a heart in a single phrase: it is a heart which neither fears God nor respects man.* This is indeed the state to which these cursed demands can bring you if you continue, as you have begun, to devote yourself totally to them, leaving no time or energy for yourself. You are wasting time and, if I may be a second Jethro, you also are exerting energy

*Ex 7:13

*Ez 36:26

*Lk 18:4

foolishly on these things which are nothing
but a spiritual affliction, a mental drain,
and a squandering of grace.* What do all   *Ex 18: 17, 18
these things produce but spiders' webs?*   *Job 8:14;
                                                    Hos 3:6

THE LIMITLESSNESS AND UNWORTHINESS
OF HIS BURDEN

III. 4. I ask you, what is the point of
wrangling and listening to litigants from
morning to night? And would that the evil
of the day were sufficient for it,* but the   *Mt 6:34
nights are not even free! Your poor body
scarcely gets the time which nature requires
for rest before it must rise for further dis-
puting. One day passes on litigation to the
next, one·night reveals malice to the next;*   *Ps 18:3
so much so that you have no time to
breathe, no time to rest and no time for
leisure. I have no doubt that you deplore
this situation as much as I, but that is in
vain unless you try to remedy it. In the
meantime, however, I urge you constantly
to beware that you never become hardened
toward the demands of your office because
of their persistence. 'I struck them and
they did not grieve,' says God.* Do not be   *Jer 5:3
like these people. On the contrary, dili-
gently adopt the disposition of the Just
Man and say with him, 'What is my
strength that I should hope? Or my end
that I should keep patience? Is my strength
the strength of stones or is my flesh like
brass?'* Patience is a great virtue, but I   *Job 6:11, 12
would hardly have wished it for you in this

2 Cor 11:19

case. Sometimes it is more commendable
to be impatient. Can you approve of the
patience of those to whom Paul said, 'You
suffer fools gladly since you yourselves are
wise'?* If I am not mistaken, this was
meant as irony and not as praise. It was a
reproach to the meekness of certain people
who had, so to speak, joined hands with
false apostles by whom they were seduced,
and had ever so patiently allowed themselves to be taken in by all the strange and
depraved teachings of those apostles. For
this reason Paul adds, 'You permit a man

2 Cor 11:20

to bring you into bondage.'* It is not the
virtue of patience to permit yourself to be
enslaved when you can be free. Do not
fool yourself; this is servitude to which you
are surely being brought as the days go by.
It is the sign of a dull heart not to sense
your own continual affliction. Someone
has said, 'Affliction makes you understand

Is 28:19

what you hear.'* This is true if affliction is
not excessive; if it is, the result is certainly
not understanding, but contempt. 'When
the wicked man sinks to the depths of sin,

Prov 18:3

he is full of contempt.'* Therefore, wake
up and not only beware, but abhor that
evil yoke of servitude which threatens you

Gal 5:1

at every moment,* or, more accurately,
which even now weighs heavily upon you.
Are you less a slave because you serve not
one but all? There is no servitude more
repulsive or oppressive than that of the
Jews which they drag after them wherever
they go. They offend their masters everywhere. But you, like them, tell me where

you can ever be free or safe or your own? Everywhere confusion and noise, the yoke of your servitude, bear down upon you.* *Ibid*

IV. 5. Do not reply now with the words of the Apostle: 'Although I was free from all men, I made myself a slave to all.'* This *1 Cor 9:19* is hardly your situation. Did Paul in his slavery aid men in the acquisition of mere financial gain? Were the ambitious, the avaricious, the simoniacal, the sacrilegious, the fornicating, the incestuous and every other kind of monstrous person crowding around him from every corner of the earth to obtain or retain ecclesiastical honors by his apostolic authority? Truly, this man for whom life was Christ and death gain,* *Phil 1:21* made himself a slave to win more for Christ,* not to increase the profits of *1 Cor 9:19* avarice. You should not, therefore, claim a precedent for your life or servitude in Paul's productive labor and in his charity, so free and unrestrained. It would be much more worthy of your apostolic office, much more beneficial to your conscience, and much more fruitful for the Church of God, if you would listen instead to another of his statements: 'You were bought for a price, do not become slaves of men.'* *1 Cor 7:23* What is more servile and more unworthy, especially for the Supreme Pontiff, than every day, or rather every hour, to sweat over such affairs for the likes of these. Tell me this, when are we to pray or to teach the people? When are we to build up the Church* or meditate on the law?** Oh

*1 Cor 14:4
**Ps 1:2*

[handwritten margin note: Corruption in the ranks of the church]

[handwritten margin note: expansion of church power — too much involvement in earthly affairs]

*Ps 18:8

yes, every day laws resound through the
palace, but these are the laws of Justinian,
not of the Lord. Is this just? Consider for a
moment. Surely, the Law of the Lord is
perfect, converting souls.* But these are
not so much laws as wrangling and sophis-
try, subverting judgment. Tell me, therefore, how can you, as bishop and shepherd

*1 Pet 2:25

of souls,* allow the Law to stand silent
before you while these others rattle on?
I am at a loss if this perversity does not
cause you anxiety. I think that sometimes
this should cause you to cry with the
Prophet to the Lord, 'Evil people have told

*Ps 118:85

me tales, but they are not like your Law.'*
Go ahead, dare to claim that you are free
even while burdened by this impropriety
which you should not endure. For if you
can be free but will not, you are a slave
even more of your own wicked will. Is he
not a slave whom wickedness governs?
Indeed he is. But perhaps you think it more
degrading for a man to dominate you than
for a vice to do so. What difference does it
make whether you serve willingly or unwillingly? Although enforced servitude is
more wretched, still, voluntary servitude is
more to be deplored. 'And what do you

*Act 9:6

want me to do?'* you ask. Spare yourself
these demands upon you. You may say this
is impossible, that it would be easier to bid
farewell to the papal throne. You would
be correct if I were urging you to break with
them rather than to interrupt them.

AN EXHORTATION

V. 6. Listen to what I condemn and to
what I suggest. If you apply all your experiences and knowledge to activity and
have nothing for consideration, do I praise
you? I do not.* Nor do I think anyone   *1 Cor 11:22
will who has heard Solomon's words, 'Who-
ever is less involved in activity will become
wise.'* Certainly, an action suffers if not   *Sir 38:25
preceded by consideration. If you want to
belong totally to all men in the likeness of
him who was made all things to all men,*   *1 Cor 9:22
I praise your devotion to mankind, but
only if it is complete. Now, how can it be
complete when you have excluded yourself? You too are a man. For your devotion
to be whole and complete, let yourself be
gathered into that bosom which receives
everyone. Otherwise, as the Lord says,
'What does it profit you to gain the whole
world, but lose yourself alone?'* Now,   *Mt 16:26
since everyone possesses you, make sure
that you too are among the possessors.
Why should you alone be cheated of your
service? How long will you be like the wind
which passes by but never returns?* How   *Ps 77:39
long will you refuse to receive yourself
with the others even when it is your turn?
You are indebted to the wise and the
foolish,* do you deny yourself alone? The   *Rom 1:14
fool and the wise man,* the slave and the   *Eccles 6:8
free man,* the rich and the poor man,**   *Eph 6:8
man and woman,† the old and the young,††   **Prov 22:2
cleric and layman, the just and the im-   †Gen 1:27
pious,* all equally share you; they all drink ††Jer 31:13
                                            *Gen 18:25

from the public fountain of your breast, and will you stand aside thirsting? If a man is cursed who squanders his own gifts, what of one who leaves them entirely untouched? Let your waters be dispersed in the street;* let men and oxen and cattle drink from them;* yes, give drink even to the camels of the sons of Abraham.* But you also drink with the others from the waters of your well.* A proverb says, 'Do not let a stranger drink from your well.'* Are you a stranger? If you are a stranger to yourself, to whom are you not? If a man is no use to himself, to whom is he useful?* Therefore, remember this and, not always, or even often, but at least sometimes give your attention to yourself. Among the many others, or at least after them, you also have recourse to yourself. What could be a greater concession? For I say this as a concession, not as a judgment. I think that I concede more in this matter than the Apostle himself.* 'Then you concede more than you ought,' you say. I do not deny it. But what does it matter, if this is what is required? I am confident that you will not be content with the instruction I hesitantly give you, but will surpass it in your generosity. It is better for you to be more generous than for me to be overly bold. In my judgment, it is safer for me to be timid than to be foolhardy before your majesty. And perhaps this is exactly how a wise man should be advised, for Scripture says, 'Give a wise man the opportunity and he will become wiser.'*

*Prov 5:16
*Jon 3:7
*Gen 24:14

*Prov 5:15

*Prov 5:17

*Sir 14:5

*1 Cor 7:6

*Prov 9:9

THE BETTER COURSE OF ACTION

VI. 7. But listen to what the Apostle
thinks about this: 'Is there no wise man
among you who can judge between bro-
thers?'* And he adds, 'I say this to shame   *1 Cor 6:5
you;* set them to judge who are most   *Ibid.
despised in the Church.'* According to the   *1 Cor 6:4
Apostle, you, as a successor of the Apostles,
are usurping a lowly, contemptible office,
which is unbecoming of you. This is why a
bishop instructing a bishop said, 'No one
who fights for God entangles himself in
secular affairs.'* However, I spare you, for   *2 Tim 2:4
I speak not of the heroic, but the possible.
Do you think these times would permit it if
you were to answer in the Lord's words
those men who sue for earthly inheritance
and press you for judgment: 'Men, who set
me as a judge over you?'* What kind of   *Lk 12:14
judgment would they soon pass on you?
'What is he saying, this ignorant, unskilled
man who is unaware of his primacy, who
dishonors his supreme and lofty throne,
who detracts from the apostolic dignity?'
And yet I am sure that those who would
say this could not show where any of the
Apostles at any time sat to judge men, to
survey boundaries, or to distribute lands. I
read that the Apostles stood to be judged,*   *Act 5:27
not that they sat in judgment. This will
happen in the future;* it has not happened   *Mt 19:28
yet. Therefore, does it diminish the dignity
of a servant if he does not wish to be
greater than his master,* or a disciple if he   *Jn 15:20
does not choose to be more than the one

*Jn 13:16

*Prov 22:28
*Lk 12:24

who sent him,* or a son, if he does not transgress the boundaries which his parents set for him?* 'Who appointed me judge?' says our Lord and Master.* Will it be wrong for his servant and disciple not to judge everything? It seems to me that a person is not a very shrewd observer if he thinks it is shameful for Apostles or apostolic men *not* to judge such things since judgment has been given to them in greater matters. Why should those who are to pass judgment in heaven even on the angels not scorn to judge the paltry worldly possessions of men?* Clearly your power is over sin and not property, since it is because of sin that you have received the keys of the heavenly kingdom,* to exclude sinners not possessors. The Lord confirms this when he says, 'That you may know that the Son of Man has power on earth to forgive sins.'* Tell me, which seems to you the greater honor and greater power: to forgive sins or to divide estates? But there is no comparison. These base worldly concerns have their own judges, the kings and princes of the world. Why do you invade someone else's territory? Why do you put your sickle to someone else's harvest? Not because you are unworthy, but because it is unworthy for you to be involved in such affairs since you are occupied by more important matters. On the other hand, where necessity demands it, listen not to me but to the Apostle: 'If this world will be judged by you, are you unworthy to judge the smallest matters?'*

*1 Cor 6:3

*Mt 16:19

*Mt 9:6

*1 Cor 6:2

∴ He should avoid judging worldly matters, but sometimes it's necessary.

VII. 8. It is one thing to rush headlong into these affairs when there is an urgent reason, but it is another, entirely, to dwell on them as if they were important and worthy of this kind of papal attention. I must express these thoughts and many like them if I am to speak forcefully, righteously and with sincerity. But since these are evil days, it is enough to have warned you not to give yourself completely or continually to activity and to lay aside something of yourself—your attention and your time—to consideration. This, however, I say more out of necessity than for the sake of justice, although to yield to necessity is not in excess of what is just.

THE NECESSITY OF CONSIDERATION

If we were permitted to do what we should, we would always, everywhere and absolutely prefer that quality which is of value in every way and cherish it alone, or at least above all else. And this is piety, as irrefutable logic demonstrates. What is piety, you ask? To take time for consideration. Perhaps you may say that I differ in my definition from the man who defined piety as worship of God.[5] But that is not so. If you carefully consider, his meaning is expressed by my words, at least partially. For what is as integral to the worship of God as that which he himself urges in the Psalm: 'Be still and know that I am God'?* This   *Ps 45:11
certainly is the essence of consideration.

What is as valuable as consideration which benevolently presumes to take part in an action by anticipating and planning what must be done?[6] This is absolutely necessary. Affairs which have been thought out and planned in advance can be accomplished efficiently, but they can lead to great danger if done haphazardly. I have no doubt that you can recall frequent experiences of this kind in legal affairs, in important business matters, or in any deliberations of significance.

Now, of primary importance is the fact that consideration purifies its source, that is, the mind. Notice also that it controls the emotions, guides actions, corrects excesses, improves behavior, confers dignity and order on life, and even imparts knowledge of divine and human affairs.[8] It puts an end to confusion, closes gaps, gathers up what has been scattered, roots out secrets, hunts down truth, scrutinizes what seems to be true, and explores lies and deceit. It decides what is to be done and reviews what has been done in order to eliminate from the mind anything deficient or in need of correction. Consideration anticipates adversity when all is going well and when adversity comes, it stands firm. In this it displays both prudence and fortitude.

VIII. 9. Since you have just seen that prudence is the mother of fortitude, and that it is not fortitude but temerity to dare something that prudence has not conceived, observe the delightful and harmonious intermingling of the virtues and how one depends on the other. Prudence is the mean of desire and necessity, and like a judge it sets definite boundaries for both. For some it provides what is needed, for others it curtails what is excessive. In this way it forms a third virtue called temperance. Consideration judges intemperate both the man who obstinately denies himself necessities and the man who indulges in excess. Thus, temperance is not only the rejection of what is excessive, but also the acceptance of what is necessary. The Apostle seems not only to have promoted this idea, but to have originated it, for he teaches us not to provide for the flesh in its desires.* Indeed, when he says not to provide for the flesh, he moderates excess; when he adds, 'in its desires,' he admits necessities. Therefore, it seems to me not altogether absurd to define temperance as a virtue which neither excludes necessity nor exceeds it. As the Philosopher says, 'Nothing in excess.'⁹

Rom 13:4

THE HARMONY OF
THE FOUR VIRTUES

10. Now concerning justice, one of the four virtues, is it not a fact that consideration guides the mind into conformity with this virtue?¹⁰ For the mind must first reflect upon itself to deduce the norm of justice which is not to do to another what

one would not wish done to himself, nor deny another what one wishes for himself.* In these two rules the entire nature of justice is made clear. But justice is not a solitary virtue. Observe its exquisite connection and coherence with temperance and likewise the relation of these two with the virtues discussed above, prudence and fortitude. Since the role of justice is said to consist in not doing to another what one does not want done to himself, the fulfillment of this virtue is expressed in the Lord's statement, 'Whatever you wish men to do to you, do to them.'* Neither of these is possible unless the will, which shapes them, is brought under control so that it neither desires anything excessive nor presumptuously avoids anything necessary. This is the role of temperance. Also, temperance sets a limit for justice in order to keep it just. The Wise Man confirms this when he says, 'Do not be excessively just.* In this way he displays disapproval of justice which is not restrained and bridled by temperance. What is more, wisdom does not refuse the bridle of temperance. With the wisdom which God gave him, Paul says, 'Do not let your wisdom go to extremes but let it be tempered by moderation.'* But on the other hand, the Lord indicates that justice is necessary for temperance; in the Gospel he censures the temperance of those who fast so they may be seen fasting by men.* There was temperance in their food, but justice was not in their hearts, because they intended not to

*Mt 7:12

*Mt 7:12

*Eccles 7:17

*Rom 12:13

*Mt 6:16

please God, but men.* And I repeat: how   *Gal 1:10*
can you have either one of these without
fortitude? It is fortitude's task, and no
small task at that, to restrain one's likes
and dislikes between the extremes of too
little and too much so that the will can be
content with this middle way which is
bare, pure, solitary, consistent and self-con-
tained, since it is equally isolated on every
side; in short, the very essence of virtue.

11. Tell me if you can, to which of
these three virtues you think we should
especially attribute the mean, which is
coterminus with them all in such a way
that it seems proper to each?[11] Or is the
mean virtue itself? But then virtue would
not be many-faceted, but all virtues would
be one. On the other hand, because no
virtue is possible without it, is the mean
somehow the essential core of the virtues
in which all are united so as to appear as
one? Certainly, they do not unite by shar-
ing it, but each totally and perfectly
possesses it. For example, what is as essential to justice as the mean? Otherwise, if
justice fails to attain the mean in all
respects, it clearly does not give to each his
due as it should.[12] Similarly, what is as
essential to temperance which is a virtue
precisely because it allows nothing in excess? But I am sure you will admit that the
mean is no less essential to fortitude,
especially since it is this virtue which
successfully rescues the mean unharmed
from the onslaught of vices which try to
strangle it, and establishes it as a solid

foundation of goodness and seat of virtue. Therefore, to maintain the mean is justice, and it is temperance, and it is fortitude. But see whether they do not differ in this way: when an undertaking is in the will, it is within the sphere of justice; it is accomplished by fortitude; and it is maintained and utilized by temperance. It remains to show that prudence is not excluded from this union. Is it not this virtue which first discovers the mean and directs the mind toward it when that middle way has been long neglected and concealed by jealous vices and covered over by the darkness of time? This is why the mean is noticed by few people, because prudence is possessed by few. Thus, justice seeks; prudence finds. Fortitude lays claim; temperance possesses. I do not intend to discuss the virtues here, but I have said this much to encourage you to set aside for consideration which leads to the discovery of these virtues and others like them. To give no time during your life to such pious and beneficial leisure, is this not to lose your life?

THE MALICE OF OUR DAYS

IX. 12. But what can you do? If you suddenly devote yourself completely to this philosophy, although it is not customary for a pope to do so, you will indeed annoy many people. You will be like a person who abandons the footsteps of his ancestors, and this will be seen as an

affront to them. You will be censured with
the common saying, 'Everyone wonders
about a person who behaves differently.' It
will seem that you only want attention.
You cannot suddenly correct every error
at once or reduce excesses to moderation.
There will be an opportunity at the proper
time for you to pursue this little by little,
according to the wisdom given you by
God.* In the meantime, do what you can   *2 Pet 3:15
to utilize other people's evil for good. If we
look for examples of good Roman Pontiffs
and not just recent ones, we will discover
some who found leisure in the midst of the
most important affairs. When Rome was
beseiged and the barbarian sword threatened
the necks of its citizens, did fear stop
blessed Pope Gregory from writing about
wisdom in leisure? At that very time, as his
preface reveals, he wrote his commentary
on the very obscure final section of Eze-
kiel.* And he did this carefully and ele-   *Homily on
gantly.   Ezekial
                                                 2:preface;
                                                 PL 76:934

X. 13. But let that be; a different custom
has developed. The times and the habits of
men are different now. Dangers are no
longer imminent, they are present.[13] Fraud,
deceit and violence run rampant in our
land. False accusors are many; a defender is
rare. Everywhere the powerful oppress the
poor. We cannot abandon the downtrodden;
we cannot refuse judgment to those who
suffer injustice.* If cases are not tried   *Ps 102:6;
and litigants heard, how can judgment   145:7
be passed?

ADVOCATES

Let cases be tried, but in a suitable manner.
The way which is frequently followed now
is completely detestable. It would hardly
suit civil courts, let alone ecclesiastical. I am
astonished that you, a man of piety, can
bear to listen to lawyers dispute and argue
in a way which tends more to subvert the
truth than to reveal it.[14] Reform this corrupt tradition; cut off their lying tongues
and shut their deceitful mouths.* These
men have taught their tongues to speak
lies.* They are fluent against justice. They
are schooled in falsehood. They are wise in
order to do evil; they are eloquent to assail
truth. These it is who instruct those by
whom they should have been taught, who
introduce not facts but their own fabrica-
tions, who heap up calumny of their own
invention against innocent people, who
destroy the simplicity of truth, who ob-
struct the ways of justice.[15] Nothing reveals the truth so readily as a simple
straightforward presentation. Therefore, let
it be your custom to become involved in
only those cases where it is absolutely
necessary (and this will not be every case)
and decide them carefully but briefly, and
to avoid frustrating and contrived delays.[16] The case of a widow requires your
attention, likewise the case of a poor man
and of one who has no means to pay. You
can distribute many cases to others for
judgment and many you can judge unworthy of a hearing. What need is there

*Ps 11:4

*Jer 9:5

to hear those whose sins are manifest
before the trial?

THE AMBITIOUS

Some people are so impudent that, even
when their case openly abounds with the
itch of ambition, they are not embarrassed
to demand a hearing. They flaunt themselves before the public conscience in a
trial where they provide sufficient evidence to condemn themselves. There has
been no one to restrain their hard-headed-
ness and therefore they have multiplied and
become even more set in their ways. I do
not understand why, but the guilty are not
shamed by the consciences of other guilty
men; where all are filthy, the stench of one
is hardly noticed. For example, are the
greedy embarrassed before their own kind,
the unclean before others like them, or the
profligate before other profligates? The
Church is filled with ambitious men; in our
age she shudders at the calculated strivings
of ambition no more than a den of
thieves shudders at the spoils taken from
travellers.*   *Mt 21:13

XI. 14. If you are Christ's disciple, let
your zeal be enflamed and let your authority rise up against the widespread plague of
this impudence. See what the Master did;
hear what he says; 'Let whoever serves me
follow me.'* He did not take time to   *Jn 12:26
listen, he took a whip to beat them. He

*Mt 21:13
*Lk 10:37

neither spoke to them nor heeded their complaints. He did not sit and judge; he pursued and punished. Still, he was not silent about the reason: they had changed a house of prayer into a place of business.* Therefore, go and do likewise.* Let such businessmen embarrass you, if that is possible; if not, give them reason to fear. You too have a whip. Let the moneychangers be afraid, and not trust in their money, but lose confidence in it. Let them hide their money from you, knowing that you are more apt to throw it away than take it. If you do this with determination and perseverance you will win many who are greedy for gain and direct them to more honorable occupations. You will also save many by preventing them from even daring to attempt this sort of thing. In addition, this will greatly increase the leisure I am urging for you. You will save a great deal of time for consideration if you refuse to deal with some business and assign some to others, and decide faithfully and with due deliberation those cases which you feel merit a hearing. I think I will add some things about consideration, but after I begin the second book. Let the first one end here so that my treatise, which is hardly pleasant, will not additionally burden you by its length.

BOOK TWO

AN APOLOGIA ON THE PLIGHT OF JERUSALEM

I REMEMBER THE PROMISE which I made to you such a long time ago, worthy Pope Eugene, and now I want to fulfill it although belatedly.[1] This delay would embarrass me, if I were aware of any neglect or disrespect on my part. But this is not the case; for we have entered a difficult period, as you well know, which appears to herald an end almost to our very existence, not to mention our endeavors. Clearly, the Lord, provoked by our sins, seems in some way to have judged the earth before the appointed time, justly, of course, but unmindful of his mercy. He neither spared his people nor his own name. Are they not saying among the nations, 'Where is their God?'* And no wonder, for the sons of the Church, and those who are called by the Christian name, lie prostrate in the desert,* slain by the sword or destroyed by hunger.* Strife has spread among the princes and the Lord makes them wander in trackless wastes.* Destruction and misery are in their paths;* fear and grief and confusion

*Ps 113:10

*1 Cor 10:5
*Lam 4:9

*Ps 106:40
*Ps 13:3

47

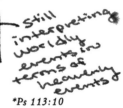

*Ps 104:30

*Is 51:7;
  Rom 10:15
*Ez 13:10

*Is 58:3

*Is 5:25

*Ex 32:12
*Ps 18:10
*Ps 35:7

*Mt 11:6

*Ps 118:52

*Cf. Ex 3:8

are in the inner chambers of the kings.* How confused are the feet of those announcing peace, of those announcing good news!* We said, 'Peace,' and there is no peace;* we promised good news, and behold there is disaster, as if we were rash or unsure in our endeavor. We rushed into this, not aimlessly but at your command, or rather, through you at God's command. Why, therefore, did we fast and he fail to notice; why did we humble our souls and he ignore us?* Indeed, 'in all of these things his anger is not turned away and his hand is still stretched out.'* Still how patiently God listens even now to sacrilegious voices and Egyptians blaspheming that he cunningly led them out to die in the wilderness?* And yet who does not know that 'the judgments of the Lord are true'?* But this judgment is so great an abyss* that, in my opinion, he is rightly called blessed who is not shocked by it.*

2. But how does the rashness of man dare to reprehend what it cannot comprehend?[2] If it is of any consolation, let us remember the judgments of God which are of old. For indeed it is said, 'I was mindful of your judgments of old, Lord, and I was comforted.'* I speak of something formerly known by all, but now known by no one. This is exactly how the human heart behaves: what we know when it is not necessary, we forget in time of need.[3] Moses, when he was about to lead the people out of the land of Egypt promised them a better land.* Indeed, for what

other reason would this people who knew only land have followed him? He led them out, but he did not bring them into the land which he had promised.* And this sad and unexpected outcome cannot be blamed on the foolhardiness of the leader. He did everything at the Lord's command and with his help, and with the Lord confirming his work afterward with signs.* 'But that people,' you say, 'was stiff-necked and always defying the Lord and his servant Moses.'* This is true enough; they were unbelieving and rebellious.* But what about the men of our day? Ask them. Why do I need to say what they themselves admit? I have one thing to say: How could they advance if they were continually turning back whenever they set out? And when during the entire journey did they not return in their hearts to Egypt?* If the Israelites fell and perished because of their iniquity,* are we astonished that today those who do the same thing suffer the same fate? But was the destruction of the Israelites contrary to the promises of God? Then neither is the destruction of our men. Indeed, the promises of God never impair the justice of God. And listen to another example.

3. Benjamin sinned.* The rest of the tribes armed for vengeance and not without the approval of God. In fact, he appointed the leader for those who were preparing to fight. And so they fought, relying on stronger forces and a more noble cause, and what is greater than all these, relying

*Deut 34: 1-5,
Cf. Num 20:12*

*Ex 7ff.
Cf. Mk 16:20*

Cf. Ex 32:9
Num 20:10

Cf. Ex 16:3

Ps 72:19

Cf. Judg 20:1 ff.

Ps 65:5

on divine favor. But how terrible God is in his counsels over the sons of men!* The avengers of the crime fled from the criminals; many fled from a few. But they ran to the Lord and he said to them, 'Attack.' They attacked again, and again they were scattered in confusion. And so just men went into a just battle, the first time with God's approval and the second time at his command, and still they failed. But as they were found inferior in battle, they showed themselves superior in faith. What do you think our men would do with me, if at my urging, they attacked again and were defeated again? When would they listen to me urging them to repeat their march a third time, to repeat the undertaking in which they had already failed a first and a second time? And yet, the Israelites did not think back over their first and second failures, but made preparation for a third time and triumphed. But perhaps our men are saying, 'How do we know this message has come from the Lord? What sign do you

Jn 6:30

make that we may believe you?'* It is not for me to answer these questions; my shame should be spared. You answer for me and for yourself, according to what you

Mt 11:4

have heard and seen,* or certainly according to your inspiration from God.

4. But perhaps you are surprised that I pursue these matters since I had proposed something else. I do this not because I have forgotten that proposal, but because I do not think these things alien to it. I remember that my discourse to you, worthy

Father, concerns consideration. Surely this
is a great undertaking and requires no
little consideration. Now, if important affairs should be considered by important
men, who is as competent as you to consider this matter, since you have no equal in
all the world? It is for you to do this according to the wisdom and power given
you from above.* Humility restrains me   *2 Pet 3:15
from writing to you that something should
be done in this way or that. It is enough
that I have intimated that something should
be done to console the Church and to close
the mouths of those who speak evil.* Let   *Ps 62:12
these few words stand as a defense, so your
conscience may have some explanation
from me with which it can excuse me and
yourself also—if not in the eyes of those
who judge actions by their results, certainly in your own eyes. A completely valid
excuse for anyone is the testimony of his
own conscience. It means nothing to me
to be judged by those who call good evil
and evil good, who substitute light for
darkness and darkness for light.* I prefer   *Is 5:20
that the murmuring of men be against us
rather than against God, if a choice must be
made. What an honor for me if he deigns
to use me for a shield. Willingly I draw to
myself the scurrilous tongues of detractors
and the poisoned darts of blasphemers so
that they do not reach him. I do not refuse
to be stripped of glory to prevent an attack
on the glory of God. Who can enable me
to glory in these words, 'For you I have
endured reproach; shame has covered my

*Ps 68:8

face?'* For me, glory is to become a companion of Christ who said, 'The reproaches of those who accuse you have fallen on me.'* Now let my pen return to the subject I had proposed for it and let my address to you proceed along its course.

*Ps 68:10

FOUR THINGS TO BE CONSIDERED
AND THE THREEFOLD CONSIDERATION OF SELF

II. 5. First of all, consider what it is I call consideration. For I do not want it to be understood as entirely synonymous with contemplation, because the latter concerns more what is known about something while consideration pertains more to the investigation of what is unknown. Consequently, contemplation can be defined as the true and sure intuition of the mind concerning something, or the apprehension of truth without doubt. Consideration, on the other hand, can be defined as thought searching for truth, or the searching of a mind to discover truth. Nevertheless, both terms are customarily used interchangeably.

III. 6. Now in order to achieve the fruit of consideration, I think you should consider four things in this order: yourself, what is below you, around you and above you. Your consideration should begin with yourself so you do not reach out to other things in vain, because you have neglected yourself. What does it profit you if you gain the whole world and lose one person—

[handwritten margin note:] This focus on self is one piece of evidence that St Bernard is one of the comparary sources to humanism.

yourself?* Even if you were a wise man
your wisdom would lack something if it
did not benefit you.* How much would it
lack? Everything, I feel. Although you
know every mystery, the width of the
earth, the height of the heavens, the depth
of the sea; if you do not know yourself,
you are like a building without a foundation; you raise not a structure but ruins.*
Whatever you construct outside yourself
will be but a pile of dust blown by the
wind. Therefore, he is not wise, whose
wisdom is no benefit to himself. The
wisdom of a wise man will benefit him*
and he will be the first to drink from the
water of his own well.* Therefore, let your
consideration begin and end with yourself.[4] Wherever it wanders, call it back to
yourself for the sake of your salvation. You
should be first and last in your own consideration. Take an example from the supreme Father of all: he sends forth his
Word and retains it. Your word is your
consideration; if it proceeds, let it not
withdraw.[5] Let it go forth but not depart;
let it leave but not desert. In acquiring
salvation, no one should be closer to you
as a brother than the only son of your
mother. Think of nothing which is contrary
to your own salvation. I should have said
'except' rather than 'contrary to.' You
must reject anything which presents itself
for your consideration that does not pertain in some way to your salvation.

IV. 7. This consideration of yourself has

*Cf. Mt 16:26

*Cf. Prov 9:12

*Cf. Lk 6:49

*Prov 9:12

*Prov 5:15

three divisions. You should consider what you are, who you are, and what sort of man you are: what you are in nature, who you are in person, and what sort of man you are in character. What you are, for example, is man. Who you are: Pope and Supreme Pontiff. What sort of man: kind, gentle, and so forth. Although the investigation of the first division belongs more to the philosopher than to the apostle, nevertheless, there is in the definition of man, whom they call a rational animal, the notion that he is mortal. And this you may look into more carefully, if you please. For there is nothing inherent in such an investigation which might stand in the way of your calling, or oppose your dignity. On the contrary, it can benefit your salvation. Now, these two, rationality and mortality, are to be considered at the same time, for it is in this way that it is beneficial. The fact that you are mortal should humble the rational in you; likewise, reason should comfort your mortality. Neither of these should be neglected in the investigation of man. If the matter at hand needs further consideration, it will be dealt with below. This will be more useful, perhaps, after all parts of the argument have been assembled.

LET HIM BE MINDFUL OF HIS FIRST PROFESSION

V. 8. Now we must turn our attention to who you are now and who you were before you were made pope. Although

I said, 'who you were before,' I suppose I
ought to omit that and leave it rather to
your reflections. I do say that it would be
unworthy of you to be less than perfect
since you have been taken from such great
perfection. Why are you embarrassed to
find yourself least among the great, when
you remember that you were great among
the least? You have not forgotten your
first profession; what is out of reach is not
out of mind or at least has not left your
heart. Your commands, your judgments
and your teachings will benefit if you do
not lose sight of that profession. This consideration makes you scorn honors in the
midst of honors. And that is a great benefit. Let it not leave your heart; it is your
shield even against that barb, 'Man in the
midst of honors did not understand.'*   *Ps 48:13*
Therefore, say to yourself, 'I was lowly in
the house of my God.* How is it that one   *Ps 83:1*
of the poor and lowly has been raised up
over nations and kingdoms? Who am I, or
what is my father's house, that I may sit
above the exalted? Surely he who said to
me, "Friend, go up higher,"* is confident   *Lk 14:10*
that I will be a friend. If I turn out to be
less than a friend, it will be of no benefit to
me. He who has raised me up can cast me
down. It will then be too late to complain,
"You lifted me up and dashed me down."*   *Ps 101:11*
High position is not designed to flatter, for
it involves greater responsibility.[6] High
position threatens danger; responsibility is
the proof of a friend. Let us gird ourselves
for this unless we want to take the

Lk 14:9

lowest place in shame.'*

WHY HE HAS BEEN ELECTED
TO THE SUPREME PONTIFICATE

VI. 9. We cannot ignore the fact that you
have been elected to the supreme position,
but, indeed, it must earnestly be asked, 'for
what purpose?' Not, in my opinion, to
rule. For the Prophet, when he was raised
to a similar position, heard, 'So that you
can root up and destroy, plunder and put
Jer 1:10   to flight, build and plant.'* Which of these
rings of arrogance? Spiritual labor is better
expressed by the metaphor of a sweating
peasant. And, therefore, we will understand ourselves better if we realize that a
ministry has been imposed upon us rather
than a dominion bestowed. 'I am not
greater than the Prophet; even if I am
equal in power, still there is no comparison
of merits.' Say this to yourself and teach
yourself, you who teach others. Think of
yourself as one of the Prophets. Is this not
enough for you? Indeed it is too much.
But by the grace of God you are what you
1 Cor 15:10   are.* What is that? Be what the Prophet
was. Or should you be more than the
Prophet? If you are wise you will be content with the measure which God has
Cf. 2 Cor 10:13   apportioned you.* For anything more than
Mt 5:37   this comes from the evil one.* Learn by
the example of the Prophet to preside not
so much in order to command as to do
what the time requires. Learn that you

need a hoe, not a sceptre, to do the work
of the Prophet.[7] Indeed, he did not rise up
to reign, but to root out. Do you think that
you also can find work to be done in the
field of your Lord? Much indeed. Certainly
the Prophets could not correct everything.
They left something for their sons, the
Apostles, to do; and they, your parents,
have left something for you. But you cannot do everything. For you will leave
something to your successor, and he to
others, and they to others until the end of
time. Still around the eleventh hour the
workers are scolded for their idleness and
sent into the vineyard.* Your predecessors,   *Mt 20:6-7
the Apostles, heard that 'The harvest in-
deed is great, but the laborers are few.'*   *Mt 9:37
Claim your inheritance from your fathers.
For 'if a son, then you are also an heir.'*   *Gal 4:7
To prove you are an heir, be watchful in
your responsibilities; do not become sluggish and idle lest it also be said to you,
'Why do you stand here the whole
day idle?*   *Mt 20:6

10. It is hardly fitting for you to be
found relaxing in luxury or wallowing in
pomp. Your inheritance[8] does not include
any of these things. But what does it
include? If you were content with its
meaning you would realize that you are to
inherit responsibility and labor rather than
glory and wealth. Does the throne flatter
you? It is a watchtower; from it you oversee everything, exercising not dominion,
but ministry through the office of your
episcopacy. Why should you not be placed

on high where you can see everything, you who have been appointed watchman over all? In fact, this prospect calls forth not leisure but readiness for war. And when is it suitable to boast, where it is not even possible to relax? There is no place for leisure where responsibility for all the churches unremittingly presses upon you.* But what else did the holy Apostle leave to you? He says, 'What I have I give to you.'* What is that? I am sure of one thing: it is neither gold nor silver; for he himself says, 'I do not have silver and gold.'* If you happen to have these, use them not for your own pleasure, but to meet the needs of the time. Thus you will be using them as if you were not using them.* These things are neither good nor bad when you consider the good of the soul, but the use of them is good, the abuse bad, solicitude for them is worse, and using them for profit is shameful. You may claim these things on some other ground but not by apostolic right.[9] For the Apostle could not give you what he did not have. What he had he gave: responsibility for the churches,[10] as I have said. Did he give dominion? Listen to him, 'Not lording it over your charge but making yourself a pattern for the flock.'* You should not think he was prompted to say this only by humility and not by truth, for the Lord says in the Gospel, 'The kings of the nations lord it over them and those who have power over them are called benefactors.'* And he adds, 'But you are not like this.'* It is clear: dominion is

*2 Cor 11:28

*Acts 3:6

*Acts 3:6

*1 Cor 7:31

*1 Pet 5:3

*Lk 22:25
*Lk 22:26

forbidden for Apostles.

11. Therefore, go ahead and dare to usurp the apostolic office as a lord, or as pope usurp dominion. Clearly, you are forbidden to do either. If you want to have both of these at the same time, you will lose both. Moreover, you should not think that you are excluded from those about whom God complains, 'They have reigned but not by me; princes have arisen but I did not recognize them.'* Now if it pleases you to reign without God, you have glory, but not before God.* But if we believe this to be forbidden, let us listen to the decree which says, 'Let the one who is greater among you become lesser, and let the one who is foremost become as a servant.'* This is the precedent established by the Apostles: dominion is forbidden, ministry is imposed. This is confirmed by the example of the Lawgiver himself who adds, 'But I am among you as one who serves.'* Who would think himself without glory if he possessed that title which the Lord of glory first applied to himself? Paul rightly glories in it saying, 'They are servants of Christ and so am I.'* And he adds, 'I speak as a fool: I am more. In many more labors, in prison more frequently, in beatings beyond measure, and often in danger of death.'* O wondrous ministry! What sovereignty is more glorious than this? If it is necessary to glory, the example of the saints is set before you, the glory of the Apostles is proposed to you. Does this glory seem insignificant to you? Who can

Hos 8:4

Rom 4:2

Lk 22:26

Lk 22:27

2 Cor 11:23

2 Cor 11:23

[handwritten margin note: Do not seek worldly glory or riches]

*Ecclus 45:2

make me equal to the saints in glory?* The Prophet cries out, 'But to me your friends, God, are made exceedingly honorable; their

*Ps 138:17

sovereignty is made exceedingly strong.'* The Apostle exclaims, 'Far be it from me to glory except in the cross of our Lord Jesus

*Gal 6:14

Christ.'*

12. I wish that you would glory always in this highest form of glory which the Apostles and Prophets chose for themselves and have passed on to you. Acknowledge your inheritance in the cross of Christ, in a multitude of labors. Happy the man who can say, 'I have labored more than

*1 Cor 15:10

all.'* This is glory, but there is nothing vain in it, nothing weak, nothing boastful. If the labor is terrifying, let the reward be an enticement. 'For each one will be

*1 Cor 3:8

rewarded according to his labor.'* Even if the Apostle has labored more than all, nevertheless he has not completed the entire task. There is still a place for you.

AN EXHORTATION TO RESPONSIBILITY AND HUMILITY

Go out into the field of your Lord and consider how even today it abounds in thorns and thistles in fulfillment of the

*Gen 3:18
*Mt 13:38

ancient curse.* Go out, I say, into the world, for the field is the world* and it is entrusted to you. Go out into it not as a lord, but as a steward, to oversee and to manage that for which you must render an

*Cf. Lk 16:1 ff.

account.* Go out, I should have said, with

footsteps of careful responsiblity and responsible care.[11] For those who were ordered to go into the whole world* did not circle the world physically, but provided for it mentally. And so, lift up the eyes of your consideration and see whether the lands are not more like fields dried for the fire than white for the harvest.* How many of the trees which you thought were fruitful, when closely inspected, will turn out to be brambles instead? In fact, they are not even brambles; they are old and decrepit trees which actually bear no fruit except perhaps acorns or husks for swine to eat. How long will they occupy the land? If you go out and see them, will you not be ashamed that your axe is lying idle, that you received the sickle of the Apostles in vain?

13. One time the patriarch Isaac went out into this field, when Rebecca first met him, and, as Scripture has it, he went out to meditate.* He went out to meditate; you must go forth to root out. You should have meditated already; the time for action is at hand. If you start to hesitate now, it will surely be too late. According to the Savior's counsel, you should have sat down beforehand to make an estimate of the task, to measure your strength, to ponder your wisdom, to reflect on the rewards of virtue, and to determine their cost.* Come, therefore, see that this is the time for pruning,[12] but only if you have already had time for meditation. If you have moved your heart, now move your tongue, and

*Mk 16:15

*Jn 4:35

*Gen 24:63

— so recognizing the pope's resp. goes beyond the personal resp. of a monk

*Lk 14:28 ff.

*Ps 44:4

*Eph 6:17
*Ecclus 36:7

*Ps 149:7–8
*Rom 11:13

*Jas 4:17

*Lk 12:47

*Heb 11:34

*Heb 11:33

also your hand. Put on your sword,* the sword of the spirit which is the word of God.* Glorify your hand and your right arm* and deal out vengeance on the nations and punishment on the peoples; bind their kings in chains and their nobles in fetters of iron.* Do this and you will honor your ministry* and it will honor you. This is no ordinary sovereignty: you must expel evil beasts from your boundaries so your flocks may be led to pasture in safety. Vanquish the wolves, but do not lord it over the sheep. You have charge over them not to oppress them but to feed them. If you have carefully considered who you are, you cannot fail to realize that this is what you should do. Furthermore, it is a sin for you to know what to do, yet not do it.* You have not forgotten where you read, 'The servant who knows his Lord's will and does not do what is proper will be beaten with many stripes.'* This was the practice of the Prophets and of the Apostles. They were mighty in war,* not weak in silks. If you are the son of Apostles and Prophets, do likewise. Justify your place in this noble lineage by acting like them, for the nobility of their line results from nothing else than the uprightness of their character and the firmness of their faith. Through this faith they conquered kingdoms, enforced justice, and obtained promises.* This is the statement of your inheritance in your father's own hand; we have unfolded it for you so you may see what portion has fallen to you.

Put on strength and you have your inheritance. Possess faith, possess piety, possess wisdom, but the wisdom of the saints
—that is, fear of the Lord*—and you have   **Ps 110:10*
what is yours. You have the entire estate of
your father without fraud. The most precious estate is virtue. A good estate is
humility on which every spiritual building
is constructed and grows into a holy tem-
ple in the Lord.* Through humility some   **Eph 2:21*
possess even the gates of their enemies.*   **Gen 22:17*
For, which of the virtues can equally sub-
due the pride of demons and the tyranny
of man? Besides, even though for everyone,
without distinction, this virtue is a tower
of strength in the face of the enemy* still   **Ps 60:4*
in some way its force is known to be
greater among great men and more re-
nowned among men of renown. No gem is
more splendid, especially as an ornament
of the Supreme Pontiff. To the extent that
he is raised higher than other men, humility
raises him above himself.

THAT HE MIGHT CONSIDER WHAT HE IS
AND WHAT IS LACKING TO HIM

VII. 14. There is a possibility that I will
be censured because the first part of my
argument had not been sufficiently developed when my pen somehow went on to
the second part, and began to describe
what sort of person you should be before
it had adequately indicated who you are. I
believe it was embarrassed because it saw a

naked man placed on so high a pinnacle and it hastened to clothe him with his insignia. For without these you will appear increasingly more unsightly as you become more famous. Can you hide the desolation of a city built on a mountaintop or the smoke of an extinguished lamp set upon a stand?* A foolish king sitting on the throne is likely a monkey on a housetop. And now, listen to my song which is beneficial, but hardly pleasant.

*Mt 5:14-15

It is a monstrous thing for the highest office to be filled with a man of the lowest character, for the first place to be occupied by a man fit for the last, for the tongue to be eloquent but the hand idle, for the talk to abound but results to be lacking, for the face to be grave but behavior capricious, for great authority to be vested in a man of faltering stability. Bring a mirror and let a dirty face recognize itself. Be glad your face is not like this. Even though there are things which you can justly be pleased with, look at yourself closely and see if there is anything which ought to displease you. I want you to glory in the testimony of your conscience,* but I also want you to be humbled by it. Rarely can a person say, 'I hold nothing against myself.'* You walk more cautiously among the good if your bad points do not lie hidden. Therefore, as I have said, know yourself, so that in the midst of these present difficulties you may draw comfort from a good conscience, but even more so that you may know your deficiencies. For who is not

*2 Cor 1:12

*1 Cor 4:4

deficient? They are totally deficient who
think they are in no way deficient. What if
you are the Supreme Pontiff? Because you
are the Supreme Pontiff are you therefore
supreme? Realize that you are the lowest if
you think you are supreme. Who is supreme? The man to whom nothing can be
added. You are in serious error if you think
you are that man. God forbid. You are not
one of those who counts honors as virtues.
You experienced virtue before honor. Leave
the other opinion to Augustus and others
who did not fear to be worshipped with
divine honors; for example, Nebuchad-
nezzar, Alexander, Antiochus and Herod.
But consider that you are called supreme
not absolutely, but in a comparative sense.
Do not think that I am speaking of a comparison of merits, but of ministries. Let
men think of you as a minister of Christ,
and—I add this without passing judgment
on anyone's sanctity—as supreme among
his ministers. For the rest, it is my wish that
you strive to be supreme, not to think you
are supreme or to wish to be thought so
before you are.[13] For how will you make
progress if you are already satisfied with
yourself? Accordingly, do not be reluctant
to discover your deficiencies or ashamed to
acknowledge them. Say with your prede-
cessor, 'It is not that I have already obtained this, or have already attained
perfection,'* and again, 'I do not claim to
have reached it.'* This is the knowledge of
the saints; this is far from that knowledge
which causes one to boast.[14] Who adds this

We've talked about papal monarchy, but Bernard does not want the pope to rule like secular monarchs

*Phil 3:12
*Phil 3:13

Eccles 1:18

knowledge adds also sorrow,* but this sorrow no wise man has ever avoided. This is a healing sorrow, through it the deadly stupor of a hardened, impenitent heart is expelled. And so he was a wise man who could say, 'My sorrow is continually before me.'* But now we must return to the discussion we have before this digression and continue with it, if there is more to be said.

Ps 37:18

HIS PERSONAL DIGNITY AND
THE PREROGATIVES OF HIS POWER

VIII. 15. Come, let us investigate even more diligently who you are; that is, what part you play in the Church of God at this time. Who are you? The high priest, the Supreme Pontiff. You are the prince of the bishops, you are the heir of the Apostles; in primacy you are Abel, in governing you are Noah, in patriarchate you are Abraham, in orders you are Melchisedech, in dignity you are Aaron, in authority you are Moses, in judgment you are Samuel, in power you are Peter, by anointing you are Christ. You are the one to whom the keys have been given,* to whom the sheep have been entrusted.* It is true that there are other doorkeepers of heaven and shepherds of flocks; but you are more glorious than all of these, to the degree that you have inherited a name more excellent than theirs.* They have flocks assigned to them, one flock to each; to you all are assigned, a single flock to a single

Mt 16:19
Jn 21:17

Heb 1:4

shepherd.* You are the one shepherd not
only of all the sheep, but of all the shepherds. Do you ask how I can prove this?
From the word of the Lord. For, to whom,
and I include not only bishops but also
Apostles, were all the sheep entrusted so
absolutely and completely? 'If you love
me, Peter, feed my sheep.'* What sheep?
The people of this or that city or region, or
even of this or that kingdom? 'My sheep,'
he said. To whom is it not clear that he did
not exclude any, but assigned them all?
There is no exception where there is no
distinction. And perhaps the rest of the
disciples were present when the Lord,
entrusting all to one man, commended
unity to all in one flock with one shepherd* according to the statement, 'One is
my dove, my beauty, my perfect one.*
Where unity is, there is perfection. Other
numbers do not possess perfection but
division, as they depart from unity. Thus it
is that each of the other apostles received a
single community, for they understood this
mystery. James, who appeared as a pillar
of the Church,* was content with only
Jerusalem, leaving to Peter the universal
Church. It was fitting for him to be placed
there to raise up offspring for his dead
brother* in the place where he had been
killed, for James was called the brother of
the Lord. Now if the brother of the Lord*
yields to Peter's prerogative, who else can
lay claim to it?

16. Therefore, according to your own
canons, others are called to share part of

*Jn 10:16

*Jn 21:17

*Jn 10:16
*Song 6:8

*Gal 2:9

*Gen 38:8

*Gal 1:19

the responsibility for souls; you are called to the fullness of power. The power of the others is bound by definite limits; yours extends even over those who have received power over others. If cause exists, can you not close heaven to a bishop, depose him from the episcopacy, and even give him over to Satan?[15] Your privilege is affirmed, therefore, both in the keys given to you and in the sheep entrusted to you. There is further confirmation of your prerogative in the gospel where the disciples were sailing and the Lord appeared on the shore, and what was a cause of greater joy—he appeared in his resurrected body. Peter, knowing it was the Lord, threw himself into the sea and thus went to him, but the others came in their boat.* What does this mean? It is assuredly a sign of the unique pontificate of Peter through which he received not just a single ship to govern, as each of the others, but the whole world. For, the sea is the world; the ships are the churches. Thus it is that, at another time, Peter walking on the waters like the Lord,* showed himself to be the unique vicar of Christ who was to preside not over a single people but over all, since: 'many waters' signifies 'many peoples.'* Thus, although each of the others has his own ship, to you is entrusted the greatest of all, made from all the others, the universal Church which is spread throughout the whole world.

*Jn 21:3 ff.

*Mt 14:29

*Rev 17:15

LET HIM CONSIDER NOT SO MUCH
WHO AND HOW GREAT HE IS
BUT WHAT KIND OF PERSON HE IS

IX. 17. Behold, this is who you are. But remember what you are. For I remember that I promised to return to this question when the opportunity arose. How opportune that when you consider who you are, you also consider what you were before! Why do I say, 'What you were before'? That is what you are even now. Why should you cease to reflect upon what you have not ceased to be? Indeed, it is one and the same thing to consider what you were and what you are, but another to consider who you have become. It is not right for this last consideration to exclude the former in the investigation of yourself. For, as I said, you are still what you were; in fact, you are what you were no less than you are pope, perhaps even more. You were born a man; you were elected a pope, you were not transformed into a pope. Your humanity has not been cast aside; the papacy has been added. Let us treat both of these at once, for I remember saying before that they both become more useful when they are compared with one another. I told you earlier that when you consider what you are, you consider the nature by which you are a man, for you were born a man.* Now, when you ask who you are, the response will be your title, which is bishop.* This is what you have been made, not what you were born.

*Book 2:8 above

*Book 2:7

Which of these seems to you to pertain more directly to your essence, what you have been made or what you were born? Is it not what you were born? Therefore, I advise you especially to consider what you especially are: what you were born, namely, man.

18. You should be attentive not only to what you were born, but also to what sort of person you are by birth, if you do not want to be cheated of the fruit and utility of your consideration. Therefore, take off these garments[16] which you have inherited and which have been cursed from the beginning. Tear off the covering of leaves which hides your shame but does not heal your wound. Destroy the pretense of this fleeting honor and the lustre of this specious glory, so you can candidly consider yourself in your nakedness,[17] for you came forth naked from your mother's womb.* Were you born wearing this mitre? Were you born glittering with jewels or florid with silk, or crowned with feathers, or covered with precious metals? If you scatter all these things and blow them away from the face of your consideration like the morning clouds which quickly pass and rapidly disappear,* you will catch sight of a naked man who is poor, wretched, and miserable.* A man grieving because he is man, ashamed because he is naked, weeping because he was born, complaining because he exists. A man born for labor, not for honor. A man born of woman and, because of this, with guilt; living for a brief

*Job 1:21

*Hos 6:4; 13:3

*Rev 3:17

time and, consequently, with fear; filled
with sorrow.* Truly, man's misfortunes are   *Job 14:1
many for they are of both body and soul.
For what calamity is missing in man, born
in sin with a frail body and a barren mind?
Man is truly filled with misfortunes in
whom an infirm body and a foolish heart
are compounded with the transmission of
sin, and condemnation to death. There is a
useful connection between thinking of
yourself as Supreme Pontiff and paying
equal attention to the vile dust which you
not only were, but are. Your thoughts
should imitate nature, and what is more
worthy, should imitate the Author of
nature, in joining what is highest with what
is lowest. Did not nature in the person of
man join the breath of life with vile dust?*   *Gen 2:7
Did not the Author of nature, in the person
of himself mix together the dust of the
earth and the Word? Thus, take your model
both from the substance of our origin and
from the mystery of redemption, so that,
seated on high, you will not be proud but
will think humbly of yourself and will be
in accord with the humble.

X. 19. Therefore, if you consider how
great you are, also ponder what sort of
man you are, and that especially. This consideration will keep you within yourself; it
will not permit you to fly from yourself, or
walk among great things which are wonder-
ful and beyond your reach.*   *Ps 130:1

LET THE MEAN HOLD FAST TO THE MIDDLE

Stand firm in yourself. Do not fall lower, do not rise higher. Do not proceed to greater length; do not stretch out to greater width. Hold to the middle if you do not want to lose the mean. The middle ground is safe. The middle is the seat of the mean, and the mean is virtue.* Every dwelling place beyond the mean is counted an exile by a wise man. Because of this, he does not dwell at a distance which is beyond it, nor in a broad way which is outside of it, nor in height above it, nor in depth below it. In fact, distance usually means exile, and broadness division, height ruin, and depth absorption. I am speaking quite clearly about this so you will not think I am talking about what the Apostle encouraged us to comprehend with all the saints: the length, width, height and depth.* These will be discussed at a later time.* Now, however, I say 'length' when a man promises himself a longer life; 'width' when the mind is extended to superfluous cares; 'height' when a man overestimates himself; 'depth' when he discredits himself too much. For example, does not the man who measures a long lifespan for himself truly set out on the path of exile, passing beyond the boundaries of life with his prolonged concern? Thus it is that men in the present are exiles from themselves through forgetfulness and pass into another time through inane concern, a time which is not profitable, indeed not even

*See above, Book 1:11

*Eph 3:18
*See below, Book 5:27 ff.

possible. Similarly, a mind stretched in
many directions must be torn by many
cares. For immoderate stretching causes
weakness and excessive weakness causes a
break. And what is haughty presumption
but a fall headlong into ruin? For you have
read: before a fall the heart is exalted.* *Prov 16:18;
What, on the other hand, is the dejection of   18:12
too much faintheartedness except over-
whelming despair? The strong man is not
depressed in this way. The prudent man is
not seduced by the uncertainty of a longer
life. The moderate man will restrain his
concerns and abstain from superfluous
cares, although he will not ignore those
that are necessary. The just man will not
presume anything higher than himself, but
will say with another man, 'If I am just, I
will not lift up my head.'* *Job 10:15

LET HIM CONSIDER WHETHER
HE IS PROFICIENT IN VIRTUE

XI. 20. Walk cautiously, therefore, in
this consideration of yourself and do so
with complete fairness so you neither attribute to yourself more than is true, nor
spare yourself more than is just. You
attribute to yourself more than is true not
only by claiming a good which you do not
possess, but even by ascribing to yourself a
good which you do possess. Distinguish
carefully what kind of person you are by
the gift of God, and let there be no deceit
in your spirit. But there will be unless

you faithfully discern and honestly assign what is yours to yourself and what is God's

*Mt 22:21

to God.* I do not doubt that you are convinced that evil is your own doing, but good comes from the Lord. Now, clearly, when you consider what kind of person you are, you must also recall what kind of person you were. Later things must be compared with earlier: have you grown in virtue, in wisdom, in understanding, in agreeableness of character, or, God forbid, have you perhaps grown weaker in these? Are you more patient or more impatient than usual, more irascible or more gentle, more insolent or more humble, more affable or more severe, more easily moved or more obdurate, more cowardly in spirit or more magnanimous, more earnest or somewhat more careless, more fearful or perhaps more confident than you ought to be? What a wide field for this kind of consideration lies open before you! I recall these few things as one who offers seeds, not as one who sows, but as one giving seed to

don't let the papacy change you

*Is 55:10

the sower.*

Reflect upon your zeal, your mercy and also your discretion which is the moderator of these same virtues. Reflect on your manner of forgiving and of avenging injuries, and in each case note how carefully you take into account means, place, and time. These three factors must certainly be considered in the practice of these virtues, for without them, they will cease to be virtues. Indeed, it is not nature but practice which produces virtues of this kind. These qualities are known to be essentially different. You can make them vices by misusing or confounding them or make them virtues by using them properly and well. When the eye of discretion is blinded, it is usual for zeal and mercy each to seize a place for itself and occupy it. Discretion is blinded by two things: anger and extreme softheartedness. The latter weakens decisions of judgment, the former pushes them to excess. How can legitimate mercy or righteous zeal fail to be endangered by either of these? An eye raging in anger sees nothing mercifully and one that is filled with a flood of womanly weakness does not see straight. You will not be innocent if you punish a man who perhaps should have been spared, or if you spare a man who should have been punished.

HOW HE OUGHT TO ACT
IN PROSPERITY AND ADVERSITY

XII. 21. In addition, I do not want you to overlook the way you act in tribulations. Be glad if you are firm in your own tribulations and sympathetic with those of others. This indicates a righteous heart. But it is the sign of a most perverse heart if you find yourself impatient in your own troubles and without compassion for those of others. What are you like in prosperity? Is there nothing here to invite consideration? Certainly there is, if you reflect diligently on how frequently a prosperous

man loosens the reins of his self-restraint
and self-discipline, at least in a small way.
As for the heedless, when did prosperity
not affect discipline as fire affects wax, or
sunshine the snow or ice? David was wise
and Solomon wiser, but the flattery of
great success made fools of them both,
the one partially, the other completely.
Great is the man who falls upon adversity
but does not fall even slightly from wisdom.
He is no less admirable who does not ridicule and mock when he has good fortune.
But it is easier to find a man who is still
wise in adversity, than one who has not
become a fool in prosperity. That man is
great and to be preferred who in prosperity
has not affected a more frivolous laugh,
more insolent speech, or more immoderate
concern for his clothes or body.

AVOIDING IDLENESS AND FRIVOLITY

*Ecclus 38:25

XIII. 22. Even if the Wise Man rightly
encourages wisdom to be written in leisure,*
idleness in leisure must be avoided. You
must flee idleness, the mother of frivolity,
and the stepmother of the virtues. Among
laymen frivolity is frivolity; in the mouth
of a priest, frivolity is blasphemy. But
sometimes if frivolous language occurs it
may have to be tolerated, but it should
never be repeated. Rather you should, with
care and prudence, interrupt it. Break in
with something serious which people can
listen to not only with profit but with

pleasure; something which can take the place of frivolity. You have consecrated your mouth to the Gospel: to open it for such trifles is unlawful, to do so frequently is sacrilege. It has been said, 'The lips of the priest are guardians of knowledge and from his mouth men seek the law'*—not frivolity or fables. It is not enough to keep from your mouth the scurrilous language which some disguise by the name of wit or urbanity. It must even be kept far from your ears. It is disgraceful for others to incite you to derisive laughter; it is more disgraceful for you to elicit such laughter from them. I cannot easily say which is more damnable: to disparage someone or to listen to disparagement.

*Mal 2:7

AVOIDING SHOWING PARTIALITY
AND EASY CREDULITY

XIV. 23. I need not wear you out with thoughts of avarice, since it is said that you value money as straw. Surely, avarice offers no cause for concern for your judgments. But there is something which is no less frequent and no less dangerous, and it habitually waylays those who judge. I do not wish you to conceal anything about this fault which may lie hidden in your conscience. Do you ask what this is? Showing partiality.* Do not think you are guilty of a small sin if you show partiality for sinners instead of judging cases on their merits. There is another vice and if you think you

(Specific to new role of the papacy)

*Rom 2:11

are free from it, in my judgment you sit
alone among all whom I have known to
ascend a throne; for truly in a singular way
you have raised yourself above yourself, as
Lam 3:28 the Prophet says. This vice is an easy cre-
dulity, a cunning little fox against whose
wiles I have found no great man sufficiently guarded. This vice is the root of
many unjustified outbursts of anger, frequent condemnation of the innocent, and
prejudice against those who are absent. But
I congratulate you and I do not fear that
you will think me a flatterer. I congratulate you, for you have presided until now
without much complaining about all these
things. And whether you are guiltless, you
alone know. Consideration must now be
given to those things which are below you.
But let this mark the beginning of a second
*See above,
Book 2:6 area of consideration* since a shorter discussion better suits the obligations of
your office.

BOOK THREE

WHAT MUST BE CONSIDERED BELOW HIM

THE PRECEDING BOOK CON-
CLUDES with a beginning for this
one. According to the proposal
made there, we must consider what is
below you. You may think you should not
ask me what this includes, most illustrious
priest Eugene. Perhaps you should ask what
it excludes. Anyone wishing to discover
what is not subject to your care must leave
this world. Your predecessors were chosen
to conquer not just some regions, but the
world itself. 'Go out into the whole world,'*   *Mk 16:15
they were told. And they sold their coats
and bought swords,* the firey word† and   *Lk 22:36
the mighty wind,¹ powerful arms from   †Ps 118:140;
God. Where did these glorious victors, these   47:8
children of outcasts not go? Where did the
sharp arrows and devouring coals of the
mighty not reach?* 'Indeed, their voices   *Ps 126:4;
have gone out to all the earth, and their   Ps 119:4
words to the ends of the world.'* Aflame   *Rom 10:18
with the fire which the Lord cast over the
earth,* their words penetrated and burned.   *Lk 12:49
These most vigorous warriors fell, but they
were not overcome; they triumphed even

79

Ps 138:17

Ps 44:17

in death. Their rule was greatly strengthened;* they were made rulers over all the earth.* You have succeeded them in this inheritance. But we must weigh with serious consideration to what extent this portion belongs to you or belonged to them. I do not think it is unconditionally yours but is subject to limitations. It seems to me that you have been entrusted with stewardship over the world, not given possession of it. If you proceed to usurp possession of it, he contradicts you who says,

Ps 49:12

'The world and its fullness are mine.'* You are not that one about whom the Prophet says, 'And all the earth shall be his posses-

Num 24:18

sion.'* That is Christ, who claims this possession for himself by right of creation, by merit of redemption, and by gift from the Father. To what other person has it been said, 'Ask of me and I will give you the nations as your inheritance and the ends

Ps 2:8

of the earth as your possession'?* Leave possession and rule to him; you take care of it.² This is your portion; beyond it do not stretch your hand.

2. 'What?' you say, 'You do not deny that I preside, yet you forbid me to rule?' This is exactly my point. It is as if he cannot preside well who presides with

Rom 12:8

care.* Is not an estate made subject to a steward and a young lord to a teacher? Nevertheless, the steward is not lord of the estate nor is the teacher lord of his lord. So also, you should preside in order to provide, to counsel, to administer, and to serve. Preside so as to be useful; preside so as to

be the faithful and prudent servant whom
the Lord has set up over his family.* For   *Mt 24:45
what purpose? So you may give them food
in due season; that is, so you may administer, not rule. Do this and as a man yourself do not strive to rule over men, so that
no iniquity may rule over you.* But this   *Ps 118:133
has been more than sufficiently treated
above where we discussed who you are.*   *Bernard refers
Nevertheless, I add this also: there is no   to Book 2:8
poison more dangerous for you, no sword
more deadly, than the passion to rule. Certainly, you may attribute much to yourself,
but unless you are greatly deceived you will
not think that you have received anything
more than stewardship from the great
Apostles.

CORRECT HERETICS, CONVERT GENTILES, CHECK THE AMBITIOUS

Remember now the statement of the
Apostle, 'I am a debtor to the wise and the
foolish.'* And if you think that this state-   *Rom 1:14
ment does not apply to you, remember this
also: the bothersome name of debtor better
suits a servant than a ruler. In the Gospel
it is a servant who hears 'How much do you
owe my master?'* Therefore, if you recog-   *Lk 16:15
nize that you are not a ruler but a debtor to
the wise and the foolish, you must take
great care and consider most vigilantly how
those who are foolish may become wise,
and how those who are wise may not
become foolish, and how those who have

lost wisdom may recover it. But in my
opinion no foolishness is more foolish than
lack of faith. Therefore, you are a debtor
to the infidel, whether Jew, Greek, or
Gentile.

3. It is important, therefore, for you to
do what you can so that unbelievers may
be converted to the faith, that converts
may not turn away, that those who have
turned away may return; moreover, that the
perverse may be directed toward righteousness, the corrupted called back to the
truth, and the corruptors refuted by invincible arguments so that they either correct their error, if that is possible, or, if it is
not, that they lose their authority and the
means of corrupting others.[3] And you
must not completely neglect the worst kind
of fools; by this I mean heretics and
schismatics, for these are the corrupted and
the corruptors. Like dogs they tear apart;
like foxes they deceive. You should make
the greatest effort either to correct such
men lest they perish, or to restrain them
lest they destroy others. Granted, time
excuses you from dealing with the Jews:
they have their boundary which cannot be
passed.* The full number of the Gentiles
must come in first.* But what do you say
about these Gentiles? Rather, what does
your consideration respond to you when
you ask such questions as the following?
Why did it seem good to the Fathers to set
limits for the Gospel and to suspend the
word of faith while unbelief was obdurate?
Why do we suppose the word which runs

*Job 14:5
*Rom 11:25

swiftly stopped short?* Who first checked
this way of salvation? Perhaps the Fathers
had a reason which we do not know, or
perhaps necessity could have hindered them.

4. What is the reason for our dissembl-
ing? With what feeling of assurance, with
what kind of conscience do we fail to offer
Christ to those who do not possess him? Or
do we restrain the truth of God in our
injustice?* Indeed, at some time it is
necessary for the full number of the Gentiles to come in. Are we waiting for faith
to fall upon them? To whom has belief
come by chance?[4] How shall they believe
without preaching? Peter was sent to Cor-
nelius* and Philip to the Eunuch;† and
if we ask for a more recent example,
Augustine, commissioned by blessed Gregory, brought the teachings of the faith to
the English. And you should follow their
examples. I add also some comments on
the obstinacy of the Greeks who are with
us and not with us; joined in faith with us,
they are separated from harmony, although
even in matters of faith they have hobbled
from the right paths.[5] Also, some comments on heresy which creeps about in
secret almost everywhere, and rages openly
among some people; for on every side in
full view, it is quick to devour the Church's
little ones. Do you ask where this occurs?
You can be sure that your legates who so
often visit the land in the South know and
can tell you.[6] They go and return through
the midst of heretics, or they pass nearby
them; but what good they have accom-

*Ps 147:15

*Rom 1:18

*Acts 10:25
†Acts 8:26

plished with them so far, we have yet to
hear. And perhaps we would have heard, if
the people's salvation were not despised for
Spanish gold.[7] It is your duty to provide a
cure for this disease.

5. But there is another foolishness
which already has rendered the wisdom of
the faith almost foolish. How has this
venom infected practically the entire Catholic Church? For even while we are in the
Church we each seek our own* and envy-

*1 Cor 13:5

ing one another and provoking one another
we are stirred to hatred, aroused in injuries,
excited to arguments; we mock deceitfully,
we are quick to slander, we burst out in
cursing, we are oppressed by the stronger
and we in turn oppress those who are
weaker. How praiseworthy for the meditation of your heart to be turned against such
an infectious foolishness which, as you
know, has seized the very body of Christ
which is the multitude of believers! O ambition, cross of those who seek after you,
how is it that you please everyone when
you torment them all? Nothing is more
excruciating, nothing more disturbing; yet
nothing is more frequented by miserable
mortals than its affairs. Today, is it not
rather ambition than devotion that wears
down the doorsteps of the Apostles? Does
your palace not resound all day with
the voices of ambition? Is it not for its
profit that all learning of the laws and
canons is sweated over?[8] Is it not for its
spoils that Italian greed longs with un-
quenchable thirst? What not only interrupts

but puts an end to even your spiritual endeavors? How often has this restless and
disquieting evil caused your holy, beneficial
leisure to be ended prematurely? It is one
thing for appeal to be made to you by the
oppressed, but another for ambition to
strive to rule the Church through you. You
must not be inaccessible to the former, nor
must you in any way give in to the latter.
How wrong it is for the ambitious to be
cherished but the oppressed spurned! You
are, indeed, a debtor to both: to the
oppressed, that you lift them up; to the
ambitious, that you restrain them.

APPEALS

II. 6. And since our discussion has
touched on appeals, it will not be irrelevant
to pursue that matter somewhat. There is
need here for an extensive and conscientious view of things lest the provisions made
for extreme necessities be rendered ineffective through abuse. It seems to me that
appeals can do great damage if not handled
with the greatest restraint. Appeal is made
to you from the whole world: this, indeed,
is in testimony of your unique primacy.
But if you are wise you will not rejoice in
the primacy but in its fruits. The Apostles
were told, 'Do not rejoice in the fact that
spirits are subject to you,'* Appeal is made   *Lk 10:20
to you, as I said, and would that it were as
beneficial as it is necessary. I wish that
when the oppressed cries out, the oppressor

*Ps 9:23

would feel it, and that the wicked would not take pride in what enrages the poor man.* What could be as fitting as this: that the invocation of your name liberates the oppressed and leaves the crafty with no refuge? On the other hand, what could be so perverse, so far from right as this: that he who has done evil rejoices, and he who bore it is needlessly harrassed? It would be most inhuman if you were not sympathetic toward the man whose affliction from the injury he had borne was increased by the effort of his journey and the burden of expenses. But it would be no less dastardly for you not to be indignant toward him who was partly the author and partly the cause of these great misfortunes. Be vigilant, man of God, when these things happen: let your compassion be aroused and also your indignation. The former you owe to the sufferer and the latter to the one causing the suffering. Let the one man be consoled by recovery of his losses, satisfaction for his injuries and an end of the false statements made against him. Let the other one be dealt with so that he repents of having done what he did not fear to do, and so that he cannot mock the punishment of the innocent.

7. I think he ought to undergo the same treatment who has appealed without cause. This formula of justice has been set before you both by the unchanging order of divine equity and, unless I am mistaken, by the law of appeals itself, so that an appeal which has been illegally made may

neither benefit the appellant nor harm the
defendant. Why should a man be harrassed
for no reason? How perfectly just that a
man injure himself when he wants to injure
his neighbor! To have appealed iniquitously
is evil; for iniquitous appeals to be made
with impunity is an incentive for their
continuance. Moreover, every appeal is
iniquitous which is not the result of a
lack of justice.

Appeal is permitted not when you want
to injure others, but when you are injured.
Appeal must be made from a court decision.
It is altogether improper for the appeal to
anticipate the court decision, unless it is a
clear case of injury. Thus, anyone who
appeals but is not injured, clearly intends
to cause injury or to gain time. Appeal is
not, however, a subterfuge but a refuge.
How many men do we know who, when
they were accused, appealed in order that,
pending a decision, they might be free to
do what is never permitted! Indeed, we
know that some people, through their
decision to appeal, have been permitted to
commit crimes all their lives, such as incest
and adultery. How is it that the very thing
which ought to be feared especially by the
depraved is protecting depravity? How long
will you ignore or turn away from the complaints of the whole world? How long will
you sleep? How long will your consideration fail to keep watch over the confusion
and abuse of appeals? Appeals are made
beyond what is just and right, contrary to
custom and order. No account is taken of

[margin note, handwritten] cautioning him against manipulations of the legal process

place, means, time, cause or person. Everywhere appeals are undertaken lightly, and for the most part with evil intent. Have evildoers not been especially terrified by appeals in the past? Now evildoers themselves by using appeals become more terrifying—even to good men. The antidote has been turned into a poison. This is not a change of the right hand of the Most High.*

*Ps 76:11

8. The evil appeal against the good so that they do not do good but refrain from it in fear of your thundering voice.* Likewise, bishops are appealed against so that they do not dare dissolve or prohibit unlawful marriages. Appeal is made against them so that they do not in any way dare punish or restrain pillaging, robberies, sacrilege, or anything of this kind. Appeal is made against them so that they cannot reject or remove unworthy and disreputable persons from sacred offices or benefices. What cure do you find for this sickness so that what was discovered as a cure may not be found lethal? The Lord was zealous for the house of prayer which had been made into a den of thieves;* do you, his minister, ignore the fact that the refuge of the unfortunate has been given over to the defense of iniquity? Can you see the aggrieved parties forestalled and those break forth to appeal who are not so much injured as wishing to injure? What secret is this? It is your duty to consider it, not mine to discuss it. 'And why,' you ask, 'do those who have been wrongly appealed against not come to demonstrate their

*Ps 103:7

*Mt 21:13

innocence and overcome malice?' I say
what is usually given in answer to this
question, 'We do not wish to be troubled
needlessly. In the Curia there are those who
readily favor the appellants and foster
appeals. If you are going to lose in Rome,
you might as well lose at home.'

9. I confess that I do not completely
disbelieve these statements. In the frequent
appeals which are made today, can you
name for me anyone who has even re-
imbursed the money for the expense of the
journey to the person against whom he had
appealed? It is certainly marvelous that all
the appellants have been found just and the
defendants found guilty by your examiners.
'Love justice you who judge the earth,'*   *Wis 1:1
he says. It is a small thing to possess
justice, if you do not also love it. Those
who possess, simply possess; those who
love burn with zeal. The lover of justice
seeks after justice and pursues it; indeed,
he persecutes all injustice. Have nothing to
do with those who think of appeals as they
think of hunting. It is a shameful saying
which has become a proverb among the
pagans, 'We have roused two fat deer.' To
put it mildly, there is more wit than
justice here.

THE ABUSE OF APPEALS

If you love justice, you do not encourage
appeals but tolerate them. But what benefit
is brought to the churches of God by your

i.e. this issue goes beyond the pope

justice, that of one man, when the opinion prevails of those who are differently disposed? But this is a matter for the place where we discuss the things which are around you.[9]

10. Now, do not think you are wasting time if you consider how you can return appeals to their legitimate use, if this is possible. And, if my opinion on this point is sought, or even cared about, I say that appeals should not be despised nor should they be utterly abused. I cannot easily say which of these is the greater excess, if not that abuse seems inevitably to induce contempt, and for this reason should be more bitterly censured since it is more harmful. Is it not true that something is more harmful which is evil in itself and worse in its effects? Does not abuse itself also weaken or destroy even the laws of nature? For, often it not only diminishes the value of even the most precious thing, but annihilates it. What are more beneficial than the sacraments? Nevertheless, when they are misused by the unworthy or unworthily administered, they are hardly beneficial; they are rather vehicles of damnation because they do not have the veneration owed to them. I admit that appeals are a great and general good for the world and that they are as necessary for men as the sun itself: truly, indeed, the right of appeal is the sun of justice* which appears and rebukes the works of darkness.

*Mal 4:2

Certainly, appeals must be fostered and safeguarded; but only those which

necessity demands, not those which cunning devises. All such appeals are abuses and
do not bring relief in time of need, but give
assistance to iniquity. Why should they not
fall into contempt? How many have even
abandoned their own rights so as to defer
in such cases and thereby not be worn out
by a long and fruitless journey? Still, many
have not tolerated the loss of what was
theirs and have dangerously scorned unjust
appeals and celebrated names.

11. Here is an example which is related
to the matters at hand. A certain man
publicly betrothed a wife. The day came for
the celebration of the wedding: everything
was ready, many were invited. And, behold,
a man coveting his neighbor's wife unexpectedly burst forth with an appeal, claiming that she had been given to him
previously and that she ought rather to be
his. The groom was stunned, everyone
pressed close, the priest did not dare proceed, all that preparation was in vain; each
returned to his own house to eat his dinner;
the bride was kept from the table and the
bed of the groom until a decision was
returned from Rome. This happened at
Paris, the noble city of the French, the seat
of the crown. Another example: in the
same city a certain man who had betrothed
a bride set the day for the wedding. In the
meantime a false charge was brought up
and certain people said they should not be
married. The case was deferred to the judgment of the Church; but without waiting
for a decision an appeal was made without

cause, without injury, and with the sole intent of deceitfully causing a delay. But the groom, either unwilling to waste what preparations he had made, or unwilling to be deprived of the company of his beloved for so long a time, proceeded with the marriage, contemning or ignoring the appeal. What about that which a certain young man presumptuously attempted recently in the church of Auxerre? For, when the holy bishop had died[10] and the clergy wished to elect another as is customary, he intervened, making an appeal and forbidding this to be done until he had gone to Rome and returned. But he did not submit that appeal. For when he saw that he was disparaged for making an unreasonable appeal, he summoned whomever he could and on the third day after the election had been held by the others, he held an election of his own.

12. And so, since it is clear from these and innumerable examples like them that abuse is not born from contempt, but contempt from abuse, what sense does it make for you zealously to punish the one almost constantly, but to ignore the other? Do you wish to restrain contempt more completely? Take care to strangle the evil seed in the very womb of its wicked mother; this will happen if abuse is punished with a fitting penalty. Remove abuse, and contempt will have no excuse. Then, the lack of an excuse will drive away anyone who might dare an abuse. Accordingly, let there be none who abuse and there will be none

who show contempt, or only a few.

You do well to refuse judgment on
appeals, or rather to refuse protection to
them, and to return many of these problems to men who are acquainted with
them, or who can more quickly become
acquainted with them. For, where the
investigation is easier and more certain,
there the decision can be safer and quicker.
How very obliging of you to spare in this
way the labors and expenses of so many
people! But you must take the greatest
care with those whom you entrust with
this task.[11]

*practical
concerns
as well as
spiritual
ones*

TRAMPLING AVARICE UNDER FOOT

I could have usefully added to these comments many more like them, but mindful
of my proposal and content to have had this
brief opportunity, I will proceed to
other matters.

III. 13. I do not think I should omit the
first thing which occurs to me. You are in
command, and uniquely. To what end?
This, I tell you, requires consideration. Is it
so you may profit from those subject to
you? Not at all, but so they may profit
from you. They made you prince, but for
their own sake, not for yours. If this were
not so, how could you think yourself
superior to subjects from whom you beg a
favor? Hear the Lord, 'Those who have
power over them are called benefactors.'*
But that refers to others. What has this to

*Lk 22:25

do with us? It would be a lie to call you a benefactor if you intend to rule over those who have been generous to you rather than to be generous to them. It is characteristic of a small, mean spirit to seek from his subjects not their improvement, but his own gain. Particularly in the person who is supreme over all, nothing is more disgraceful. How appropriately the Teacher of the Gentiles advised that parents should store up wealth for their children, not children for their parents!* That same Apostle's statement deserves no small glory: 'I do not seek a gift, but fruit.'* But now let us leave this subject so that no one interprets my lingering in these matters as an indication of avarice in you; for I testified in the second book how far removed from avarice you are.*

I know how much you have rejected and how great your need is. Thus, I have written these things for you, not because of you. Surely, what is written to you should not profit you alone. This place in my work attacks avarice and from this vice your reputation is sufficiently safe; whether your work is also is your own affair.* Nevertheless, to say nothing of the offerings from the poor which you do not allow to be touched, we have seen German sacks shrink not in content but in value. Silver was reckoned as straw: the pack horses, although their packs were not lightened, unwillingly returned home with their burdens intact. What a revolution! When had Rome ever before returned gold? Even

*2 Cor 12:14

*Phil 4:17

*See Bk 2:23

Meant to be a broader treatise?

*Mt 27:4

now we do not believe this was undertaken
on the advice of the Romans. Two men
came, both rich, and both accused. Now,
one was from Mainz, the other from
Cologne. To the one acquittal was granted
freely. The other, whom I believe was
unworthy of being acquitted, heard, 'You
will leave wearing the same garment you
entered with.'* What a commendable senti- *Ex 21:3*
ment, truly in accord with apostolic liberty! Is it any less than saying, 'Your money
perish with you'?* No, except that zeal is *Acts 8:20*
primarily expressed in the second, moderation in the first. What about the man who
traveled across land and sea from a country
beyond the sea, almost from the ends of
the earth, to buy a bishopric a second time
with other people's money as well as his
own? Indeed, he had already bought it
once. He brought much, but he took it
back; not all of it, however. The poor
fellow fell into the hands of others more
able to receive than to give. You did well
to keep your hands blameless on both
these counts: namely, not agreeing to lay
them on the ambitious, or to place them
under the riches of an evil man. You did
not hold back from the poor bishop, giving
so that he might give, so he would not be
branded as miserly: he received secretly
what he gave openly. Thus, from your
purse the man's shame was provided for;
thus also, through your beneficence he gra-
tified the Curia and avoided the ill-will of
those who love gifts. You cannot hide it:
we know what happened and the person

involved. Does it bother you to hear this? The more annoyed you are to hear this the more willingly do I proclaim it. If the former is expedient for you, so is the latter for me. It is as fitting for me not to keep silent about the glory of Christ as it is for you not to seek your own glory.* And if you proceed to murmur still, the Gospel will give you an answer, 'The more he charged them, the more they proclaimed him saying, "He has done all things well".'*

*Jn 7:18

*Mk 7:36-37

PRELATES, IMPATIENT OF SUBMISSION, SEEKING INDEPENDENCE

IV. 14. Listen to another point; if, indeed, it is another. For, someone may perhaps say it pertains to the same point. Your consideration will decide this. Anyone who may think that this should be classified as a species of avarice seems to me not far from the truth. In fact, I would not deny that it is either a species of that vice, or has a similar appearance. Clearly, it is important to your perfection that you avoid evil things as well as things which appear evil. In the one you show regard for your conscience; in the other for your reputation. Consider whatever is off-color as unlawful for you, even if otherwise it may be lawful. Finally, ask your predecessors, and they will say to you, 'Abstain from all appearance of evil.'* Surely, the minister of the Lord should imitate the Lord, for he says, 'Who serves me, let him follow me.'*

*1 Thess 5:22

*Jn 12:26

And you have concerning him, 'The Lord has reigned, he is clothed with majesty; the Lord is clothed with strength.'* You also should be strong in faith, majestic in glory, and you will show yourself an imitator of God.* Your strength is the confidence of a trustworthy conscience; your majesty, the splendor of a good reputation. So, I entreat you, put on strength, for the joy of the Lord is your strength.*

In fact, he delights in the beauty of your appearance no less than if it were his own likeness that caused him delight. Put on the garments of your glory,* clothe yourself in the double garments with which that virtuous woman used to clothe her servants.[12] When your conscience is free from the faltering weakness of a lukewarm faith, and your reputation from notoriety, you are clothed in double garments, 'and the groom will rejoice over his bride, your soul, and your God will rejoice over you.'[13] Do you wonder where this is leading? Are you still unaware of what I wish to say? I will not keep you in suspense any longer; I speak of murmuring complaint of the churches. They cry out that they are being mutilated and dismembered. There are none, or only a few, who do not suffer the pain of this affliction, or live in fear of it. Do you ask what affliction this is? Abbots are freed from the jurisdiction of bishops, bishops from that of archbishops, archbishops from that of patriarchs or primates. Does this seem good? I wonder whether this practice can even be excused. In doing this you

*Ps 92:1

*Eph 5:1

*Neh 8:10

*Is 52:1

*[margin handwritten note: Similar to what he says to the knights *Is 52:1* (in terms of heavenly v. earthly glory)]*

demonstrate that you have the fullness of power, but perhaps not of justice. You do this because you have the power; but the question is whether you ought to do it. You have been appointed, not to deny, but to preserve the degrees of honor and of dignities and the ranks proper to each, as one of your predecessors says, 'Render honor to whom honor is due.'*

Rom 13:7

15. The spiritual man is one who judges all things so that he is judged by no one.* He will precede every undertaking with a three-fold consideration: first, whether it is lawful; second, whether it is suitable; last, whether it is also advantageous.* Even if it can be established, in Christian philosophy at least, that nothing is suitable unless it is lawful, and that nothing is advantageous unless it is suitable and lawful, nevertheless, it does not necessarily follow that all that is lawful will be suitable or advantageous. Come, let us apply these three criteria to the present situation. But how can it not be unsuitable for you to make your will the law, and to exercise power with no regard for reason, since there is no one to whom your actions can be appealed? Are you greater than your Lord* who says, 'I have not come to do my will'?* Still, it is no less characteristic of a debased spirit than of a haughty one, to act not from reason but from whim, to be moved not by judgment but by passion, as if devoid of reason. What is so bestial? And if it is unworthy of anyone with the use of reason to live as an animal, who can bear

*1 Cor 2:15

*Cf. 1 Cor 6:12

*Jn 13:16

*Jn 6:38

such an affront to nature, such an injury
to honor, in you, the ruler of all? By sink-
ing to such a state, and I wish it were not
so, you have brought on yourself the
general reproach, 'Man, when he was in
honor, did not understand; he resembles
the senseless beasts and has become like
them.'* What can be so unworthy of you   *Ps 48:13*
as to hold everything, yet not to be content with it, unless you can strive in some
way to make your own the trifles and insignificant elements of all that has been
entrusted to you—as if they were not yours
already? In this connection also, I want
you to recall the parable of Nathan about
the man who had a hundred sheep and yet
desired one which belonged to a poor
man.* On this point also, remember the   *2 Sam 12:1-7*
deed, or rather the crime, of King Achab,
who possessed supreme power but strove
to obtain a single vineyard.* May God   *1 Kings 21:2 ff.*
spare you what Achab heard, 'You have
slain and you have taken possession.'*   *1 Kings 21:19*

16. I do not want you to offer me the
result of these exemptions as an excuse;
indeed, the only result is that bishops become more insolent and monks even more
dissolute. And what about the fact that
they even become poorer? Look carefully
at the property and the lives of those who
have been liberated all around to see
whether the poverty of the former and the
worldliness of the latter are not totally
shameful. These are the twin progeny of a
pernicious mother, liberty. Why should a
wandering and wrongly liberated throng

not sin more freely, since there is no one to censure it? Also, why should an unarmed monastery not be more freely plundered and pillaged, since there is no one to defend it? Where, indeed, is their refuge? Is it with the bishops, grieving over their injury? Indeed, they look on with eyes of ridicule whether the monks commit evils or suffer them. What profit at all is there in that blood?* I fear that which God threatened in the Prophet, saying, 'He shall die in his iniquity; but I will demand his blood from your hand.'* How is he innocent who grants the exemption, if the one who is exempted is haughty and the one from whom he is exempted is enraged? But this is put too weakly. We are involved with a conflagration. Listen to a more candid account. If the one who murmurs is spiritually dead, how is the one who incites him alive? Furthermore, how is he not guilty of the death of both—and of his own death also—who provided the sword with which both were killed? This is the point I tried to make when I said, 'You have slain and you have taken possession.'* Besides, those who hear these things are scandalized; they are indignant and cry out and blaspheme—that is, they are wounded mortally. It is not a good tree which produces such fruit:* arrogance, dissoluteness, dissipation, deception, scandal, hatred, and what is cause for greater grief, serious hostility and continuous discord among the churches. You see how true this statement is, 'All things are lawful for me, but not all are

*Ps 29:10

*Ezek 3:18

*1 Kings 21:19

*Cf. Mt 7:17

advantageous.'* What if it happens that this   **1 Cor 6:12*
is not lawful? Forgive me, but I am not
easily convinced that this is lawful which
produces so many unlawful results.

17. Can you be of the opinion that it is
lawful for you to cut off the churches from
their members, to confuse the order of
things, to disturb the boundaries which
your predecessors have set?* If the role of   **Prov 22:28*
justice is to preserve for each what is his,
how can it befit a just man to take from
each what belongs to him?[14] You are
wrong if you think your apostolic power,
which is supreme, is the only power insti-
tuted by God. If you think this, you dis-
agree with him who says, 'There is no
power except from God.'* Equally, what   **Rom 13:1*
follows, 'Who resists the power, resists the
ordinance of God.'* Even though this is   **Rom 13:2*
principally on your behalf, it is not solely
on your behalf. The same one also says,
'Let every soul be subjected to higher
powers.'* He does not say 'to a higher   **Rom 13:1*
power' as if in one person, but 'to
higher powers' as if in many. Therefore,
yours is not the only power from God;
there are intermediate and lesser ones. And
just as those whom God has joined to-
gether must not be separated,* so those   **Mt 19:6*
whom God has made subordinate must not
be made equal. You create a monster if
you remove a finger from a hand and
make it hang from a head, above the hand
and on a level with the arm. So it is in the
body of Christ if you put members in places
other than where he arranged them. Unless

you think it was another who placed
'some in the Church as apostles, some as
prophets, others as evangelists, others as
teachers and pastors, for the perfection of
the saints, in the work of the ministry to
Eph 4:11-12   build up the body of Christ.' And this is
the body which Paul himself describes for
you with his truly apostolic eloquence:
'he adapts the whole body most suitably
to its head and represents it as closely
joined and knit together through every
joint of the system according to the func-
tioning in due measure of every single part
and deriving its increase through building
Eph 4:16   up itself in love.' You should not think
this form is to be despised because it is on
earth; it has an exemplar in heaven. For the
Son cannot do anything unless he sees the
Jn 5:19   Father doing it; especially since it was said
to him under the name of Moses, 'See that
you make everything according to the
pattern which was shown to you on the
Heb 8:5   mountain.'

18. He had seen this who said, 'I saw
the holy city, the new Jerusalem, coming
Rev 21:2   down from heaven, prepared by God.'
Now I think this was said for the sake of a
comparison: just as in heaven the Seraphim
and Cherubim, and each of the other ranks,
down to the angels and archangels, are
arranged under one hand, God;[15] likewise,
here on earth the primates or patriarchs,
archbishops, bishops, priests or abbots, and
all the rest are arranged under one supreme
Pontiff. It must not be thought insignificant
that this order has God as its author, and

derives its origins from heaven. But if a
bishop should say, 'I do not want to be
under the archbishop,' or an abbot, 'I do
not want to obey the bishop,' this is not
from heaven. Unless perhaps you have
heard any of the angels saying, 'I do not
want to be under the archangels,' or someone from one of the lesser ranks saying that
he refused to be subject to anyone but
God. You respond, 'What! Do you forbid
me to dispense?' No, but to dissipate. I am
not so ignorant as not to know that you
have been set up as a dispensor, but this
was to build not to destroy.* Moreover,
'It is required among dispensors that a man
be found faithful.'* Where necessity demands, a dispensation is excusable; where
utility requires it, a dispensation is praiseworthy. But this utility must be common
to all, not for the sake of one. But when
neither of these reasons is present, it is
clearly not the dispensation of a faithful
man, but an instance of obvious dissipation. But, who is unaware that situated in
various dioceses there are some monasteries
which have belonged in a special way to the
Apostolic See from their very foundations
by the wish of their founders. But there is
a difference between a privilege granted to
devotion and one which ambition, impatient of restraint, strives to obtain. Indeed,
this is all I will say about these matters.

*2 Cor 10:8

*1 Cor 4:2

CONSIDER HOW THE APOSTOLIC ORDINANCES
ARE TO BE PRESERVED
IN THE UNIVERSAL CHURCH

V. 19. It remains for your consideration to be vigilant over the whole state of the universal Church to see whether the people are humbly obedient to the clerics as they should be; whether the clerics are to the priests; whether the priests are to God; whether in monasteries and religious houses order is maintained and discipline observed; whether evil deeds and false doctrines are vigorously censured by the Church; whether the vineyard blossoms with honorable and holy priests;[16] whether these flowers bear fruit, the obedience of faithful people;* *Song 7:12 finally, whether your apostolic decrees and regulations concerning them are observed with fitting diligence so that there is nothing in the field of the Lord which is uncultivated out of neglect or uprooted by deceit. Have no doubt such a situation can occur. Even if I exclude the many, in fact innumerable, instances of neglect present everywhere, I can easily point out some endeavors, even among those planted by your right hand,* which have been repudiated. *Ps 79:16 Did you not promulgate with your own mouth the laws proposed at the Council of Rheims?[17] Who observes them? Who has observed them? You deceive yourself if you think they are observed. If you do not think this, then you have sinned either by decreeing what cannot be observed or by neglecting the fact that your decrees are not observed. You said, 'We command that neither bishops nor clerics should offend those who see them, and whose model and example they ought to be, through extravagance, a disgraceful array of colors, the cut of their clothing, or the style of their hair; but rather, that by their actions they condemn errors and by their manner of living they demonstrate their love of innocence, just as the dignity of the clerical order demands. But if those who have been warned by their bishops do not comply within forty days, let them be deprived of their ecclesiastical benefices by the authority of those same bishops. Furthermore, because no one is more responsible for the faults of subordinates than lazy, negligent masters, let bishops who have failed to impose the stipulated penalty abstain from the episcopal office until they do impose upon the clerics subject to them the punishment established by us. Also, we command this should be added: no one is to be ordained archdeacon or dean except a deacon or a priest. Moreover, if archdeacons, deans, and provosts who are below the orders just mentioned are disobedient and refuse to be ordained, let them be deprived of the honor they have received. On the other hand, we forbid the aforesaid honors to be conferred on young men or those beneath the rank of holy orders, unless they are distinguished by their prudence and their worthy lives.'

20. These are your words; you have sanctioned them. What effect have they

had? Young men and those who are beneath the rank of holy orders are still promoted in the Church. As for the first law: luxury in dress was condemned, but not stopped; punishment was prescribed, but hardly enforced. It has now been four years since the time when we heard the decree issued, and still we have mourned no cleric[18] deprived of his benefice and no bishop suspended from his office.[93] But the consequence of all this is cause for bitter sorrow. What is it? Impunity: the child of negligence, the mother of arrogance, the root of insolence, the nurse of transgression. And blessed are you if you endeavor with the greatest diligence to beware of negligence, the primogenitor of all evils. But pay attention and lift up your eyes now and see whether multicolored garments do not still disgrace the clerical order,[20] and whether enormous openings in their clothing do not all but reveal their groins as much as before. It is their practice to say, 'Does God care about dress and not about morals?' But this form of dress is indicative of deformity of mind and morals. Why do clerics wish to be one thing and to appear another? Indeed, this is hardly virtuous and hardly honest. Actually, by their dress they show themselves to be knights; by their profession, clerics; by their behavior, neither. For, they neither fight as knights nor preach as clerics. To what order do they belong? When they desire to belong to both they abandon both and confound both. 'Every one,' he says, 'shall rise in his

own order.'* And these, in what order shall
they rise? Will they perish without an order
who have sinned without an order?* Or, if
the supremely wise God is truly thought to
have left nothing without order from the
heights to the depths, I fear they will be
ordered to the place where no order dwells,
but only eternal horror.* O how the bride
must be pitied who is entrusted to such
attendants, who do not fear to keep for
their own profit what was assigned for her
adornment! Truly, they are not friends of
the groom, but are rivals.

And this is sufficient concerning what is
below you, if not in respect to the abundance of material, which is excessive, at
least in respect to that which I proposed.
The things which are around you are yet
to be examined, but the fourth book will
open the door to these matters.

*Cf. 1 Cor 15:23

*Rom 2:12

*Job 10:22

BOOK FOUR

I F I HAD BEEN MORE FULLY AWARE of the manner in which you received the books previous to this, most loving Eugene, I would have proceeded accordingly either with greater confidence or greater caution, or I might, indeed, have stopped altogether. Now, surely, since the distance between us allowed no opportunity for this, you should not be surprised if this dangerous address is somewhat inadequate—I shamefully admit it—as it comes to the center of this discussion.

Since the first points for consideration were treated in the earlier books, we must now include those things which are around you. These are really below you, but inasmuch as they are closer, they are more troublesome to you. Indeed, situated in your presence they cannot be neglected, concealed, or forgotten. They press upon you more violently; they attack you more tumultuously. They cause fear that you will be overwhelmed. I do not doubt that you have learned sufficiently from your own experience what need there is for sober, intent consideration of these things.

Otherwise, if careful and timely consideration does not intervene, you will continually be occupied and your trouble will be without limit and your anxiety without end. You will have no leisure; your heart will not be free. You will labor more and accomplish less. I am talking about the daily pressure you feel from the City, from the Curia, and from your household.[1] These, I say, are around you: your clergy and your people. You are in a special way their bishop and are, therefore, bound by a special obligation to care for them. And these include those who attend you daily, the elders of the people, the judges of the world, and also those who share your house and table: chaplains, chamberlains and the minor officials assigned to various duties in your service. These associate with you more intimately, disturb you more frequently and are more annoying in the trouble they cause you. These are they who are not afraid to wake the beloved, even before she wishes.*

Song 2:7

THE BEHAVIOR OF THE CLERGY
AND THE ROMAN PEOPLE

II. 2. First of all, these clergy should be very well ordered, for they especially set the example for clergy throughout the whole Church. Furthermore, every offense which is perpetrated in your presence is more disgraceful for you. It is important for the glory of your holiness that those

whom you have in your sight be ordered
and organized in such a way that they be a
model and mirror of all honor and order.
They above all others should be prompt in
fulfilling their duties, worthy to administer
the sacraments, concerned for the peoples'
instruction, careful to maintain themselves
in all purity.

What shall I say about the people? They
are the Roman people. I cannot express my
feelings about the people of your diocese
more briefly or more forcefully. What has
been so well known to the ages as the arrogance and the obstinacy of the Romans?[2]
They are a people unaccustomed to peace,
given to tumult; people rough and intract-
able even today and unable to be subdued
except when they no longer have the means
to resist. Behold your affliction: its care
rests with you; it is not right for you to
neglect it. Perhaps you laugh at me, per-
suaded that it is incurable. Do not despair:
care is required of you, not a cure. You
have heard, 'Take care of him'* and not   *Lk 10:35
'Cure,' or 'Heal him.' Indeed, someone
has said, 'It is not always possible for the
doctor to heal the sick.'* But even better,   *Ovid, Epistola
I offer you something from one of your   ex Ponto
                                                  1:3:17
own. Paul says, 'I have labored more than
all.'* He does not say, 'I have achieved   *1 Cor 15:10
more than all,' or, 'I have produced greater
results than all,' but very scrupulously he
avoids an arrogant word. Moreover, the
man whom God taught knew that each one
would receive according to his labor,* not   *1 Cor 3:8
according to his results. And, therefore, he

*2 Cor 11:23

thought man should glory in his labors rather than in his achievements, just as you have him saying elsewhere, 'In many more labors.'* And so, I say, you do your part and God will take care of his satisfactorily without your worry and anxiety. Plant, water, be concerned, and you have done your part. To be sure, God, not you, will

*1 Cor 3:6-7

give the growth when he wishes.* Whenever he does not wish it, it costs you nothing, as Scripture says, 'God will reward the

*Wis 10:17

labors of his saints.'* The labor is secure, for no failure can vitiate it. And I have said this without prejudice to divine power and goodness. I know the hardened heart of this people, but, 'God is able to raise up

*Mt 3:9
*Jon 3:9
*Is 6:10

children to Abraham out of these stones.'* Who knows but he may return and forgive,* relent and heal them?* But it is not my intention to tell God what he should do; would that I could convince you of what you ought to do and how you ought to do it!

3. But the course of my argument has become rough and uncertain. For as soon as I rise to say what I am thinking I can anticipate what will happen: anything I say will be decried as an innovation, for it cannot be denied that it is just. However, I would not even agree that my position is an innovation. Indeed, I know that it was once customary, and from this state it could fall into disuse; but to revive it would not be an innovation. For will any-one deny that a thing is customary which is known not only to have been done

once, but to have been repeated over a long period of time? I could state what this is but there would be no point. Why? Because it will not please the satraps* who favor majesty more than truth. There were those before you who devoted themselves completely to feeding their sheep, glorying in the work and in the name of shepherd, counting nothing unworthy of them except what they thought was a hindrance to the safety of the sheep. They were not self-seeking* but unsparing, unsparing of their care, their wealth, and themselves. Whence one of them says, 'I will gladly be spent for your souls.'* And as if they had said, 'We did not come to be served, but to serve,'* they presented the Gospel without charge as often as was necessary.* The only profit they sought from their subjects, their only glory, their only desire was in some way to be able to prepare them as perfect people for the Lord.* They devoted every effort to this, even in great suffering of heart and body, in labor and hardship, in hunger and thirst, in cold and nakedness.*

4. Where, I ask, is this custom now? A very different one has sprung up; interests have changed drastically and I only wish it were not for the worse! Nevertheless, I admit care and anxiety, rivalry and worry persist: they are transferred, not diminished. I bear witness to you that you do not withhold your wealth any more than your predecessors. However, the difference lies in your perverse expenditures. What a great abuse! Few look to the mouth of the

*1 Sam 29:6

*1 Cor 13:5

*2 Cor 12:15
*Cf. Mt. 20:28

*1 Cor 9:18

*Lk 1:17

*2 Cor 11:27

lawgiver, all look to his hands. But not
without reason: they carry out all the
papal business. Whom can you name from
all this great City who received you as Pope
without a reward or the hope of one? When
they offer service, then especially do they
wish to rule. They promise to be loyal so
they can better harm the faithful. Because
of this you will have no deliberation from
which they think they should be excluded,
no secret into which they will not intrude.
If the doorkeeper makes anyone of them
delay outside your door, even for a short
time, I would not want to be in his place.
And now from a few examples judge
whether I am at least somewhat acquainted
with the practices of this people. Above all
they are wise to do evil,* but they do not
know how to do good. They are detested
on earth and in heaven, they are hostile
toward both; irreverent toward God, dis-
respectful toward holy things, quarrelsome
among themselves, envious of their neigh-
bors, discourteous to strangers. Loving no
one, no one loves them; and since they
strive to be feared by everyone, they must
fear everyone. These are men who do not
endure subjection, who do not know how
to command; they are unfaithful to su-
periors, insupportable to inferiors. These
are brazen in asking, shameless in denying.
These are insistent to receive, restless until
they do, ungrateful when they have. They
have taught their tongues to say grand
things, although their deeds are paltry.
They are most generous in their promises,

*Jer 4:22

but most sparing in their gifts; they are
fawning in flattery and biting in slander;
they are blatant liars and wicked traitors.
We have proceeded this far thinking you
should be fully and clearly warned about
such people inasmuch as they are among
those things which are around you.

5. Now let us return to the order of the
work. How is it that those who say to you,
'Well done, well done,'* are bought with   *Ps 39:16*
the spoils of the churches? The life of the
poor is sown in the streets of the rich. Silver
glistens in the mud; people run to it from
every direction and it is picked up not by
the man who is more in need but by
the stronger, or by the one who happens to
run faster. Nevertheless, this custom, or
rather this sickness, did not begin with
you; I only wish it would end with you!
But let us go on to the rest. In the midst of
all this, you, the shepherd, go forth adorned
with gold and surrounded by colorful
array.* What do the sheep receive? If I dare   *Ps 44:10*
say it: this is more a pasture for demons
than for sheep. Doubtless Peter engaged in
the same practice, and Paul amused himself thus! You see the entire zeal of the
Church burn solely to protect its dignity.
Everything is given to honor, little or
nothing to sanctity. If, when circumstances
require, you should try to act a little more
humbly and to present yourself as more
approachable, they say, 'Heaven forbid! It
is not fitting; it does not suit the times; it is
unbecoming to your majesty; remember the
position you hold.' Pleasing God is their

very last concern. There is no hesitation for the loss of salvation, except that they confuse what is exalted with what is helpful to salvation, and whatever smells of glory, this they call just. All that is humble is felt to be shameful among the courtiers such that you can more easily find someone who wishes to be humble than someone who wishes to appear so. Fear of the Lord is thought simple-mindedness, not to say foolishness. They condemn as a hypocrite the circumspect man and the man who is the friend of his own conscience. Moreover, they say he is useless who loves quiet and who sometimes gives himself leisure.

LET HIM GIVE THE EXAMPLE

III. 6. What are you doing about this? Are you as yet on your guard against those who have surrounded you with the snares of death?* I implore you, endure a little more and bear with me. Rather, forgive me not so much for saying these things indiscreetly as for saying them timidly. I am jealous of you with a jealousy that is good,* and would that it were as useful as it is vehement. I know where you dwell;* unbelievers and subversive men are with you. They are wolves, not sheep; but still you are the shepherd of such men. It is useful for you to consider how you might find a way—if this is possible—to convert them, so they do not subvert you. Why do we doubt that they can be changed back

*Ps 17:6

*Cf. 2 Cor 11:2
*Rev 2:13

into the sheep from which they were
turned into wolves? Here, indeed, I do not
spare you, in order that God may spare
you. Either deny openly that you are the
shepherd of this people or show it by your
actions. You will not deny it unless you deny
you are the heir of him whose throne you
hold. This is Peter, who is known never to
have gone in procession adorned with either
jewels or silks, covered with gold, carried
on a white horse,[3] attended by a knight or
surrounded by clamoring servants. But
without these trappings, he believed it was
enough to be able to fulfill the Lord's
command, 'If you love me, feed my
sheep.'* In this finery, you are the suc-   *Cf. Jn 21:15*
cessor not of Peter, but of Constantine.[4]
I suggest that these things must be allowed
for the time being, but are not to be
assumed as a right. Rather, I urge you on
to those things to which I know you have
an obligation. You are the heir of the
Shepherd and even if you are arrayed in
purple and gold, there is no reason for you
to abhor your pastoral responsibilities:
there is no reason for you to be ashamed
of the Gospel.* If you but preach the   *Rom 1:16*
Gospel willingly you will have glory even
among the Apostles. To preach the Gospel
is to feed. Do the work of an evangelist
and you have fulfilled the office of
shepherd.*   *Cf. 2 Tim 4:5*

7. 'You instruct me to feed dragons
and scorpions, not sheep,' you reply. Therefore, I say, attack them all the more, but
with the word, not the sword. Why should

you try to usurp the sword anew which you were once commanded to sheathe?* Nevertheless, the person who denies that the sword is yours seems to me not to listen to the Lord when he says, 'Sheathe your sword.'* Therefore, this sword also is yours and is to be drawn from its sheath at your command, although not by your hand. Otherwise, if that sword in no way belonged to you, the Lord would not have answered, 'That is enough,'* but, 'That is too much,' when the Apostles said, 'Behold here are two swords.'* Both swords, that is, the spiritual and the material, belong to the Church; however, the latter is to be drawn for the Church and the former by the Church. The spiritual sword should be drawn by the hand of the priest; the material sword by the hand of the knight, but clearly at the bidding of the priest and at the command of the emperor.[5] But more of this elsewhere.[6] Now, take the sword which has been entrusted to you to strike with, and for their salvation wound, if not everyone, if not even many, at least whomever you can.

8. You respond, 'I am not better than my fathers.* Which of them has this rebellious house not ridiculed, let alone listened to?' If that is the case, continue to persevere. Perhaps they will listen and be at peace.* Persevere even if they resist. Because I say this, perhaps I will be called excessive. But was it our voice which said, 'Welcome, or unwelcome, be insistent'?* Call this excessive if you dare. The Prophet

*Jn 18:11

*Ibid.

*Lk 22:38

*Ibid.

*1 Kings 19:4

*Ezek 3:11

*2 Tim 4:2

is commanded, 'Cry out unceasingly.'* Against whom, unless against criminals and sinners? He says, 'Show my people their transgressions, the house of Jacob their sins.'* Note carefully that they are called both criminals and the Lord's people. Keep this in mind about them also: even if they are criminals, even if they are wicked, be careful that you do not hear, 'What you did not do for one of my people, neither did you do for me.'* I admit that until now this people has been hard-headed and obstinate;* but I do not know how you can be sure whether in fact they are indomitable. What has not yet been can be in the future. You may doubt, but 'with God nothing will be impossible.'* If they are hard-headed, harden yourself also against them.* Nothing is so hard that it does not give way to something harder. The Lord says to the Prophet, 'I made you even harder than their hardness.'* The one thing which absolves you is this: if you have acted toward these people so you can say, 'My people, what should I have done for you and did not do?'* If you have done this and have made no progress, one thing still remains for you to do, 'go forth from Ur of the Chaldees,'* and say, 'I must spread the Gospel to other cities also.'* I do not think you will regret your exile when you have exchanged the world for the City.

*Is 58:1

*Ibid.

*Mt 25:45

*Ezek 3:7

*Lk 1:37

*Ezek 3:8

*Ibid.

*Cf. Mic 6:3

*Gen 15:7

*Lk 4:43

WHAT KIND OF MEN HE OUGHT TO CHOOSE
AS HIS COLLEAGUES AND ASSISTANTS

IV. 9. Let us come to your colleagues
and assistants. These men are working on
your behalf and are intimate with you. For
this reason, if they are good they are
especially good for you. If they are evil,
then likewise they are more than evil for
you. You would not be called healthy if
your side were wounded; so, you should
not be called good if you rely on evil
associates. Or, if you should be good, what
fruit can be produced by your goodness
alone? I recall I have said this in the
preceding book.* What advantage, I ask,
does your justice—that of one man—give
the churches of God when a contrary
opinion prevails? But your own goodness
is not safe when beseiged with evils, any
more than your health is, with a snake
nearby. There is no place to which you can
escape from an internal evil. On the other
hand, good within your household is all
the more beneficial because it is more avail-
able. But who is more to blame than you
whether they lighten your burden or increase it, since you have chosen these men
or at least admitted them? I am not speaking of everyone for there are some whom
you have not chosen, but they you. But
they do not have power unless you either
give it to them or permit them to have it.
And thus we are back to the same point.
Blame yourself for whatever you suffer
from one who can do nothing without you.

*Book 3:9

Enough has been said about those who already hold positions, but as for the others, you see that you must be considerate in choosing or assembling them for the work of this ministry. It is your duty to follow Moses' example* and to summon from everywhere, and to associate with yourself, not youths, but elders, men who are old not so much in age but in virtue, men whom you recognize as the elders of the people.* Must they not be chosen from the whole world who are to judge the world? Certainly, such office is not to be had for the asking; appointment must be made by deliberation, not request. There are inevitably some things which petitioners importune from us or merit by their needs. But this applies to things which are ours. What right does a petitioner have when I am not permitted to do what I want, unless the petitioner forms his request in such a way that I am permitted to do what he asks, and not in such a way that I should desire to do more than is lawful for me? Some ask on another's behalf, and some ask on their own behalf. A man on whose behalf you are petitioned should be suspect; the one who petitions for himself is already judged. It does not matter whether someone petitions in person or through another. You can be sure that a cleric who frequents the Curia but is not a member of it belongs to the same class of self-seekers. Put in the same class with petitioners the man who flatters and speaks so as to please everyone, even if he asks for

Ex 3:16

Num 11:16

nothing. It is not the face of the scorpion that you should fear, he stings with his tail!

10. If you feel your heart soften at the flattery of such men, as is normal, remember what is written, 'Every man sets out his good wine first and when men have drunk freely, then that which is worse.'* Place the same value on the humility of him who fears and of him who hopes. It is customary for a shrewd and treacherous man to make a pretense of humility when he wishes to obtain something. About such men Scripture says, 'There is one who humbles himself wickedly but inwardly he is full of deceit.'* From your own experience take a clear and familiar example of this statement. How many whom you have received as humble have you afterwards put up with as troublesome, insolent, quarrelsome, and rebellious! Indeed, the evil they hid at first was afterwards revealed. Do not regard a loquacious youth practiced in eloquence as anything but an enemy of justice if he is void of wisdom. About false brothers of this kind the Master says to you, 'Do not be quick to lay hands on anyone.'*

11. And so, when you have excluded all such pestilent men, be very careful to bring in men whose presence you will not later regret. It is unseemly for you very often to retract what you have done and it is not proper for your judgment frequently to be put in peril. Accordingly, with care personally investigate everything which

*Jn 2:10

*Ecclus 19:23

*1 Tim 5:22

must be done and discuss it with those who
love you. Investigate before a thing is done
because afterwards it will be too late to re-
examine it. The advice of the Wise Man is,
'Do all things with counsel and afterwards
you will not be sorry.'* About those who
are to be admitted, convince yourself of
this: it is difficult for them to be tested
once they are in the Curia. Therefore, if
possible, proven men should be chosen and
not those who have yet to be proven. We in
the monasteries accept all men with the
hope of improving them; but the Curia
usually accepts good men more easily than
it makes men good. But if we have shown
that in the Curia more good men have
weakened than evil men have improved,[7]
certainly men must be sought in whom
neither failure is feared nor growth is
hoped for, since they are already perfect.

*Ecclus 32:24;
cf. RB 3:13*

12. Therefore, take in not those who
wish office or who run after it, but those
who hesitate and those who decline it; even
force them and compel them to enter.*
I think your spirit will find rest among such
men who are not impudent, but modest
and respectful; besides God alone they
fear nothing, they hope for nothing except
from God. They look not to the hands of
those who approach, but to their needs.
And they manfully stand up for the afflicted and judge fairly for the meek of the
earth.* They are men of suitable character,
proven sanctity, ready obedience, and quiet
patience. They are subject to discipline,
severe in censuring, catholic in faith,

Lk 14:23

Is 11:14

faithful in service; inclined toward peace, and desirous of unity. These are men who are upright in judgment, farsighted in counsel, prudent in commands, industrious in organization, energetic in actions, modest in speech. Such men are fearless in adversity, faithful in prosperity, sober in zeal, not remiss in mercy. They are not idle in their leisure, not dissolute in hospitality, not extravagant in entertainment. They are not anxious in the care of their own property nor eager for that of another; they are not prodigal with their own possessions but are everywhere and in all things circumspect. Whenever necessity arises and they are commanded to be ambassadors for Christ,* they do not refuse; but they do not strive for such office when they are not commanded to do so. They do not obstinately reject what they modestly refuse. When they are sent, they do not go after gold* but follow Christ.† They do not regard the ambassadorship as a source of gain, nor do they seek profit, but results.* They present themselves as John to kings,* Moses to the Egyptians,* Phineas to fornicators,* Elijah to idolaters,† Elisha to the covetous,* Peter to liars,† Paul to blasphemers,* and as Christ to those who traffic in holy things.**They do not despise common people but teach them; they do not flatter the rich but terrify them; they do not burden the poor but look after them; they do not fear the threats of princes but scorn them. Such men neither enter with commotion nor depart in anger.

*2 Cor 5:20

*Ecclus 31:8
†Mt 16:24

*Phil 4:17

*Mt 14:4

*Ex 5:1 ff.

*Num 25:6-9
†1 Kings 16-40
*2 Kings 5:20-27
†Acts 5:1-11
*Acts 13:45-46;
  18:6
**Mt 21:12-13

They do not despoil the churches but repair them. They do not empty pockets but renew spirits and correct faults. They are careful about their own reputations but do not envy another's. They habitually devote themselves to prayer, and in every undertaking place more confidence in it than in their own industry or labor. Their arrival is peaceful, their departure unassuming. The speech of such men is edifying,* their lives are just; their presence is pleasing, their memory is blessed. They make themselves lovable not by their words but by their deeds;* they inspire awe by their acts not by their disdain of others. They are humble with the humble and innocent with the innocent.* They refute the harsh harshly, restrain the wicked, and give the proud what they deserve.* They do not hasten to enrich themselves or their friends from the dowry of the widow[8] and the patrimony of the Crucified. They give freely what they have freely received;* freely they do justice for those who bear injustice;* they wreak vengeance on the nations and chastisement on the peoples.* They seem to have received your spirit, as the seventy received the spirit of Moses,* and by it whether absent or present they strive to please you, to please God.* They return to you weary indeed, but not stuffed with bounty. They return boasting not that they have brought anything curious or precious from the lands of their travels, but that they have left behind them peace for the kingdoms, law for the barbarians,

*Eph 4:29

*Cf. 1 Jn 3:18

*Ps 17:26

*Ps 93:2

*Mt 10:8

*Ps 102:6
*Ps 149:7

*Num 11:16

*Cf. 2 Cor 5:9

quiet for the monasteries, order for the
churches, discipline for clerics, a people
acceptable to God and zealous for good
works.*

*Tit 2:14

V. 13. It may be fitting to interject the
story of our beloved Martin of blessed
memory.[9] You know it, but I do not know
whether you remember it. He was a cardinal priest who, after serving as legate in
Dacia for some time, returned so poor that
he scarcely arrived at Florence because his
finances were almost depleted and his
horses exhausted. There the bishop of the
place gave him a horse which carried him as
far as Pisa where we were at the time. I
think it was the next day when the bishop,
who had followed, began to solicit help
from his friends, for he had a suit with an
adversary and the day of the hearing had
arrived. And when he had solicited each of
them he came to Martin. The bishop had
all the more confidence in him since Martin
could not have forgotten his recent favor.
But Martin said, 'You have deceived me; I
did not know your case was pending. Take
your horse; he is there in the stable.' And
he returned the horse to him that same
hour. What do you say, my Eugene? Is it
not an event from another century: that a
legate has returned from the land of gold
without gold, that he has traveled through
the land of silver and not known silver,
and above all that he has immediately
returned a gift which could have
been suspect?

14. What a delight it is for me to have occasion to recall and to mention a man, the memory of whom is most pleasant, I speak of the bishop, Geoffrey of Chartres, who at his own expense vigorously administered the legation to the regions of Aquitaine, and for so many years![10] I speak of something I saw myself. I was with him in that land when a certain priest presented him with a fish which they commonly call a sturgeon. The Legate asked how much it cost and said, 'I do not accept it unless you accept payment.' And he gave five solidi to the reluctant and shame-faced priest. Another time, when we were in a certain village the lady of that village as a sign of reverence offered him with a towel two or three dishes which were beautiful even though made of wood. This man of scrupulous conscience examined them for some time and praised them, but he did not agree to accept them. When would he have accepted silver dishes who refused wooden ones? There were none who could say to this Legate, 'We have enriched Abraham.'* *Gen 14:23* Indeed, with Samuel he used to declare freely to all, 'Speak of me before the Lord and before his Anointed, whether I have taken any man's ox or ass, whether I have defrauded anyone, whether I have oppressed anyone, whether I have accepted a bribe from any man's hand, and this day I will despise it and return it to you.'* *1 Sam 12:3* O that there might be an abundance of such men as this one was and as those were whom we described to you before him! What

could bring greater happiness to you, what could bring more joy to this age? Would not the happiness of these times seem to you second only to that of eternity if you could see yourself surrounded wherever you went by such an illustrious multitude of saintly men?

15. If I know you, you are hesitating and, with a deep sigh, are saying to yourself, 'Do you think what is said can happen? Do you think we will be here when these things occur? Who can make us live so we can see it? Oh, if I could see in my lifetime the Church of God supported by such columns! Oh, if I could see the spouse of my Lord commited to such faith, given over to such purity! What greater blessing for me, what greater reassurance, than to see men of this kind around me as guardians of my life and at the same time witnesses to my life? To these men I might safely commit my every secret, communicate my plans, pour myself out totally as if to another self. And if I should ever wish to stray, they would not permit me; they would restrain me from impulsive actions, they would rouse me from inaction; their respect, freely given, would repress my haughtiness and correct my excesses; their unwavering strength would sustain my doubts and encourage me in despair; their holiness and faith would summon me to whatever is holy, whatever honorable, whatever is modest, lovable and of good re-

pute.'* And now, my Eugene, redirect your eyes to the present state of the Curia and of the Church, and to the pursuits of the prelates, especially of those who are near you.

16. But that is enough on this topic. I have only touched the surface; I have not dug into the wall. You may dig into the wall and see, as the son of the prophet did.* I must proceed no further. I will say one thing, which is no secret: it is ridiculous for your ministers to try to place themselves before your fellow-priests.[11] Reason does not support this practice, nor does tradition, and no authority agrees with it. And if some pretence is offered on behalf of this practice, better, indeed, that it be condemned than the exalted order of the priesthood. But their reason for especially desiring this preferment is quite frivolous. They say, 'It is we who stand nearest the lord Pope for all celebrations, we sit next to him when he is seated, and in processions we immediately precede him.' None of this is the privilege of rank, but is a requirement of diligence, for in your solemn ministrations you fulfill the name of deacon.[12] Finally, when the priests are arranged, according to their rank, around his Majesty you sit at his feet. You are positioned closer to be prepared better to serve. We read in the Gospels that there was strife among the disciples over which of them seemed the greater.* How happy you would be, Eugene, if everything else around you were held in such esteem!

*Ezek 8:8-9

*Lk 22:24

HOW HE SHOULD PRESIDE
OVER HIS HOUSEHOLD

VI. 17. I am weary of the Curia now. We should leave the palace; they are waiting for us at home where they are not only around you, but in a certain way within you. It is not a useless consideration by which you endeavor to order your house and provide for those who are close to your heart.[13] I say it is even a necessary consideration. Listen to Paul: 'If anyone does not know how to rule his own house, how will he care for the Church of God?'* *1 Tim 3:5* And again, 'If anyone does not provide for his relatives, and especially his own family, he has denied the faith and is worse than an unbeliever.'* *1 Tim 5:8* And saying this, I do not advise you, occupied as you are with matters of the greatest importance, to direct your attention to insignificant affairs and as it were reduce your sphere of influence, or to expend on trifles what you owe to affairs of importance. Why should you entangle yourself in those concerns from which God delivered you? He says, 'All these things shall be yours as well.'* *Mt 6:33* Nevertheless, you ought to have done these without neglecting the others.* *Mt 23:23* But while personally attending to important matters it is also required that you personally provide men to oversee lesser matters on your behalf. For if one of your servants cannot himself simultaneously guard your horses and care for your table, how can you yourself equally attend to your house and the

Lord's about which is written, 'O Israel,
how great is the house of the Lord'?*   *Baruch 3:24
Certainly, a mind occupied with so many
important matters ought to be without
the worry of minor, insignificant concerns.
It should be free so no business can forcibly
make a claim on its attention. It should be
upright so no unworthy attachment can
drag it down. It should be righteous so no
evil intention can turn it aside. It should be
cautious so no suspicion can furtively
enter it. It should be vigilant so no curious,
wandering thought can distract it. It should
be firm so no sudden disturbance can shake
it. It should be invincible so no tribulation,
even if it be continuous, can exhaust it. It
should be expansive so no temporal loss
can constrain it.

18. Do not doubt that you must be
deprived of all these goods and afflicted
with evils if you divide your attention and
wish to devote it equally to the things of
God and to your trivial affairs. You must
find someone whom you can engage to
grind for you. I say 'for you' not 'with
you.' Some things you will do by yourself,
some things together with others, and some
things through others without yourself.
'Who is wise and will understand these
things?'* Your consideration should not   *Hos 14:10
fall asleep among these things. I should
think the affairs of your house must be
placed in the last category I mentioned.
You will tend to them, as I said, through
another. But if he is not faithful he will
cheat; if he is not prudent, he will be
cheated. Therefore, a faithful and prudent

*Mt 24:45

man must be sought whom you can set over your household.* He is still useless if a third thing is lacking. Do you ask what this is? Authority. For what good is it for him to want to dispose everything as is necessary and to know how to, if he is not able to do what he knows how to do and wants to do? Therefore, he must be given the ability to do what he pleases. If you think it is unreasonable to do this, remember nevertheless that he is faithful and will wish to act reasonably; recall that he is prudent and will know how to act reasonably. But a faithful and wise man is profitable only when he has sufficient support to allow the full realization of his capacity, and when everyone obeys without hesitation. Everyone, therefore, must be subject to this man. Allow no one to oppose him. Let there be no one who says, 'Why did you do this?' Let him have the power to exclude and to admit whom he wants, to change ministers, to transfer offices to whomever he wants, whenever he wants. Let him be feared by all so he may also be of use to all. Let him be in charge of all so he may benefit all in every way. Do not listen to secret, whispered accusations against him; rather, think of them as slander. And I wish that you would make this a general rule for yourself, that you hold suspect everyone who fears to say openly what he has whispered in your ear. But if in your judgment a thing should be said openly and he refuses, judge him to be not a plaintiff but an informer.

19. Therefore, let one man assign duties
to all, and let all answer to that one. And
you should have faith in him so you can be
free for yourself and the Church of God. If
you can find only a faithful man or one
who is prudent, the former must be preferred. Certainly, this is the safer alternative. But if you do not find a suitable man,
I advise you to bear with a man who is even
less faithful rather than immerse yourself in
this labyrinth. Remember, the Savior had
Judas as his overseer.* What is worse for a   *Jn 12:6
bishop than to devote himself to his fur-
nishings and paltry possessions, to scrutinize everything, to inquire about each item,
to be tormented by gnawing suspicions, to
be upset at each loss or instance of
neglect? I say this to shame certain men of
this kind who daily scrutinize their every
possession, numbering every item and demanding an account to the last penny.[14]
That Egyptian did not act this way, who
gave everything over to Joseph and did not
know what he had in his own house.* The   *Gen 39:6
Christian should blush who does not trust
a Christian with his property. A man without the faith had faith, nevertheless, in
his servant, giving him authority over all
his goods*—and this servant was a foreigner.   *Mt 24:47
20. A strange situation! Bishops have
more than enough people on hand to whom
they can entrust souls, but they find no
one to whom they can commit their paltry
possessions: obviously they have made the
best evaluation of the situation—they have
great concern for the least matters, little

or no concern for the greatest. But as we are clearly given to understand, we more patiently bear Christ's loss than our own. Each day we carefully review the expenses of the day, but are unaware of the continual losses of the Lord's flock. There is a daily dispute with the servants concerning the price of food and the number of loaves of bread; rarely indeed is a meeting convened with the priests concerning the people's sins. An ass falls and there is someone to raise her up; a soul perishes and there is no one who gives it a thought. It is no wonder, since we certainly do not sense our continual failings. Are we not angered, aroused, troubled by each computation of our expenses? How much more tolerantly ought we have sustained the loss of material goods than of spiritual! Paul says, 'Why not rather be defrauded?'* Please, you who teach others, teach yourself,* if you have not already done so, to value yourself above your possessions. Those things are transitory and can in no way remain with you; see that they pass from you, not through you. A stream hollows out the land where it flows; so, the flow of temporal things erodes the conscience. If a torrent can rush into the fields without damaging the crops, be confident that you can deal with these things without injuring your soul. I exhort you to use every means to avert from yourself the onslaught of these things. Remain unaware of many things, neglect even more, and forget about some.

21. There are, however, some things of

*1 Cor 6:7
*Rom 2:21

which I would not want you to be ignorant:
the character and the pursuits of each
person in your house. You should not be
the last to know their faults, which we
know has very often happened. And, therefore, as I said, let one person manage one
thing and another person another, but you
provide for discipline; entrust that to no
one. If a word sounds insolent to you or
anyone's deportment appears insolent, raise
your hand against insolence and avenge
your injury. Impunity produces daring;
daring produces excess. Sanctity befits the
house of a bishop,* as do moderation and   *Ps 92:5
honor; discipline is their guardian.

The servants of a priest are either more
honorable than others, or are subjects of
gossip to all. Allow nothing disgraceful,
nothing improper to remain in the appearance of those who are around you, or in
their deportment or their demeanor. Let
your fellow bishops learn from you not to
have boys with luxuriously curled hair and
foppish young men in their retinue. Surely,
youths with curled hair do not belong
among men who wear the mitre. And remember what the Wise Man warns: 'Do
you have daughters? Do not show them
your cheerful face.'*   *Ecclus 7:26

22. Still, I do not urge austerity upon
you, but gravity. The former causes the
weak to flee; the latter restrains the frivolous. The former, if it is present, renders
you hateful; the latter, if it is absent, renders you contemptible: but in all things
moderation is best. I would not want you

to be too strict or too lax. What is more
pleasing than this moderation whereby you
are not a burden by your strictness, nor
an object of contempt by your familiarity?
In the palace show yourself Pope; at home
show yourself the father of your household. Your servants should love you; if
not, see that they fear you. A guard over
your lips is always useful, but not one that
excludes gracious affability. Therefore, an
impulsive tongue must be bridled everywhere, but especially at social gatherings. If
indeed you would actually be strict, that
deportment is most suitable which is serene
in appearance and guarded in speech. The
chaplains and those who are continually
with you at Divine Office should not be
without honor. It is your duty to provide
yourself with such men as are worthy. Let
these be served by everyone just as you
are. Let them receive what they need from
your hand. Let them be content with those
things which you provide for them; and
you see that they are not in need. If you
should catch anyone seeking more than
this from strangers, judge Gehazi![15] The
same judgment must be passed on doorkeepers and the rest of the officials. But
this is superfluous; for we remember that
this rule of conduct was already formulated by you some time ago. What could
be more worthy of your apostolate? What
could be more healthful for your conscience, more fitting for your reputation,
more useful as an example? It is an excellent canon which rejects the gain obtained

through oppression,* that is, not just in   *Is 33:15*
conscience but in actual fact.

EPILOGUE AND ADDENDA

VII. 23. We can bring this book to a
close now, but here at the end, as an epilogue, I would like either to repeat some
things which have been said before, or to
add some things which have been omitted.
Before everything else, you should consider
that the Holy Roman Church, over which
God has established you as head, is the
mother of churches, not the mistress;[16]
furthermore, that you are not the lord of
bishops, but one of them, and the brother
of those who love God and the companion
of those who fear him.* For the rest, con-   *Ps 118:63*
sider that you ought to be a model of
justice, a mirror of holiness, an exemplar
of piety, a preacher of truth, a defender of
the faith, the teacher of the nations,* the   *1 Tim 2:7*
leader of Christians, a friend of the Bride-
groom,* an attendant of the bride, the   *Jn 3:29*
director of the clergy, the shepherd of the
people, the instructor of the foolish,* the   *Rom 2:20*
refuge of the oppressed, the advocate of
the poor, the hope of the unfortunate, the
protector of orphans, the judge of widows,*   *Ps 67:6;*
the eye of the blind,* the tongue of the   *cf. Lk 18:2-8*
    Is 29:18
mute,† the support of the aged,* the   †Is 35:6
    Tob 5:23
avenger of crimes, the terror of evil men,
the glory of the good, the staff of the
powerful,* the hammer of tyrants, the   *Ps 109:2*
father of kings, the moderator of laws, the

*Mt 5:13
*Jn 12:46
*Gen 14:18
*1 Sam 26:9
*Ex 7:1

*2 Tim 2:7

*Ps 33:17
*Ps 17:16

dispenser of canons, the salt of the earth,* the light of the world,* the priest of the Most High,* the vicar of Christ, the anointed of the Lord,* and, finally, the god of Pharoah.* Understand what I am saying: the Lord will give you understanding.* When power is joined to evil intent, you must assume for yourself something above your humanity. Let your countenance be against those who do evil.* Let him fear the spirit of your anger,* who does not fear man, who is not terrified by the sword. Let him fear your prayers, who scorns your warnings. Let him with whom you are angry think that God, not man, is angry with him. Let him who will not listen to you fear that God will listen to you speaking against him. The discussion has now come to things which are above you; with God's help I hope to treat these in one book and thereby fulfill my promise.

BOOK FIVE

THOSE THINGS WHICH ARE ABOVE HIM

THE FORMER BOOKS, although they are entitled 'On Consideration,' nevertheless contain many things which pertain to action, for they teach or advise some things which must not only be considered but acted upon. However, the book at hand will deal with consideration alone, for those things which are above you, our present topic, require not action, but examination. There is no way in which you can act upon those things which always exist in the same way and which will be the same for all eternity (some of these have even been the same from all eternity). And I would wish, most wise Eugene, that you be intelligent enough to realize that your consideration wanders whenever it turns from these things to lesser, visible things, whether they be regarded as a source of knowledge, or sought for practical application, or administered and employed officially. However, if your consideration deals with these things so that through them it seeks what is above, it does not go into exile: to consider in this way is to return to one's homeland. That is a more sublime and more worthy use of present things when, according to the wisdom of Paul, 'the invisible things of God are clearly seen through the things that have been made.'* Clearly, exiles, not citizens, need this ladder. The author of this statement himself recognizes this for when he said that the invisible is seen through the visible he expressly added 'by the creature of the world.'* Truly, what need is there of a ladder for one who already holds the throne? The creature of heaven already possesses the means through which he can contemplate invisible things. He sees the Word, and in the Word he sees what has been made through the Word.* He has no need to beg knowledge of the Maker from the things which have been made.* Nor does he descend to them even in order to know them, for he sees them there where they are far better than they are in themselves. Consequently, he does not require the medium of a bodily sense to reach them: he is his own sense and he senses them themselves. The best kind of vision occurs when you are self-sufficient and need nothing in order to know everything you wish to know. Moreover, to be assisted from without is to become dependent and this is to be less than perfect and less than free.

2. Why do you need anything, especially from inferiors? Is this inversion not unworthy of you? It is clearly degrading for a superior to require the service of

*Rom 1:20

*Ibid.

*Cf. Jn 1:3

*Ibid.

an inferior, although no man will be perfectly free of such degradation until he has escaped into the liberty of the sons of God.* They, indeed, shall all be taught by God† and shall all be made happy by God alone without the intervention of any creature. This will be a returning home: to have left the land of the body for the region of the spirit, which is our God, the supreme spirit, the most sublime dwelling of blessed spirits. Let the bodily sense, the imagination, not usurp for itself anything here, for here is Truth, here is Wisdom, Virtue, Eternity, the Supreme Good. For the time being we are absent from this place and where we are is a valley, a valley of tears,* in which sensuality rules and consideration is in exile. Here the bodily senses exert themselves freely and forcefully but the eye of the spirit is shrouded in darkness. Is it a surprise, then, if the stranger needs the help of the native? And happy is life's pilgrim who can turn the kindness of these citizens to his service (without it he cannot accomplish his pilgrimage), using them, but not enjoying; impelling but not seeking; demanding not begging.

Rom 8:21
†Jn 6:45

Ps 83:7

THREE SPECIES OF CONSIDERATION
FOR ASCENDING

II. 3. He is great who is satisfied to use the senses as if they were the wealth of those citizens and to employ them for his own salvation and that of others. And he is no less great who uses philosophy to establish the senses as a step toward invisible things. The latter is more pleasant, the former more beneficial; the latter more delightful, the former more courageous, But he is greatest of all, who, scorning the use of sensible objects insofar as is possible to human frailty, has accustomed himself occasionally to soar in contemplation to the sublime, not by gradual steps but by sudden ecstasies. I think the ecstasies of Paul are of this last type: ecstasies, not ascents, for he says he was 'caught up,' not that he ascended.* For this reason he said, 'If we are beside ourselves, it is for God.'* Moreover, these three occur together when consideration, even in the place of its exile, is strengthened by the efforts of virtue and the assistance of grace and either restrains sensuality so it does not grow haughty, or constrains it so it does not stray, or flees it so it cannot corrupt. In the first instance, consideration is more powerful, in the second more free, in the third more pure: indeed, that flight is made with wings of purity and ardor.

2 Cor 12:2

2 Cor 5:13

4. Do you wish these kinds of consideration to be distinguished by their own name? If it is acceptable, let us call the first consideration practical, the second scientific, the third speculative.[1] The definitions will indicate the rationale behind these names. Consideration is practical when it uses the senses and sense objects in an orderly and unified manner to win God's

favor. Consideration is scientific when it prudently and diligently scrutinizes and ponders everything to discover God. Consideration is speculative when it recollects itself and, insofar as it is aided by God, frees itself for the contemplation of God. I think you are aware that this is the fruit of the other two and that if they are not related to it, they are not what they seem to be. The first kind of consideration, without an awareness of the last, sows much and reaps nothing. Unless the second kind directs itself toward the third, it moves but does not advance. So then, what the first wishes, the second smells and the third tastes. However, the other two also lead to this same taste, although the first arrives more laboriously, the second more quietly.

THREE WAYS BY WHICH OUR CONSIDERATION INVESTIGATES GOD AND THE ANGELS

III. 5. You say, 'You have spoken enough about the route of this ascent; you have also to speak about that to which one must ascend.' You are mistaken if you hope for this; it is ineffable. Do you think I am going to say what eye has not seen, and ear has not heard, and what has not entered into the heart of man?* The Apostle says, 'God has revealed it to us through his Spirit.'† Therefore, what is above is not taught through words but is revealed through the Spirit. Truly, what words do not explain, consideration seeks, prayer

*1 Cor 2:9

*1 Cor 2:10

aspires to, life merits, purity attains, Indeed, when I remind you of those things
which are above, do not think I am telling
you to look up at the sun, the moon, the
stars, or the firmament itself, or the waters
Ps 148:4 which are above the heavens. All these
things, although superior in location, are
inferior in value and natural worth, for
they are corporeal. Your portion is spirit
and you seek in vain for something in any
way superior which is not spirit. God is
Jn 4:24 spirit and the holy angels are spirit, and
these are above you. But God is superior by
nature, the angels by grace. You and the
angels have one excellence: reason. But
God possesses no one thing which is
excellent, he is wholly and completely
excellent. He and the blessed spirits who
are with him must be investigated by our
consideration in three ways—as if by three
avenues of approach—opinion, faith and
understanding. Of these, understanding
relies on reason, faith on authority and
opinion is supported only by a semblance
of truth. Two of these possess certain
truth: but that of faith is hidden and
obscure, that of understanding is bare and
manifest. Opinion, on the other hand,
possesses no certainty but seeks truth
through what appears true rather than
grasping hold of it.

6. Above all we must avoid confusion
so that faith does not fasten onto the uncertainty of opinion or opinion call in
question what is firm and fixed in faith.
Know well that opinion is foolhardy if it

asserts something, and faith is weak if it
hesitates;   likewise   understanding   is
reckoned an intruder, a searcher of ma-
jesty,* if it tries to break the seal of faith.   *Prov 25:27
Many have thought their opinion to be
understanding and have been wrong. Indeed, opinion can be thought understanding, but understanding cannot be thought
opinion. How can this be? Because opinion
can be mistaken; understanding cannot, for
if it could be mistaken it would not be
understanding, but opinion. For, true understanding has not only certain truth, but
knowledge of the truth. We can define
each of these as follows: faith is a kind of
voluntary and sure foretaste of truth not
yet evident; understanding is a sure and
manifest knowledge of something not seen;
opinion is to hold something as true which
you do not know to be false. Therefore, as
I said, faith possesses nothing which is
uncertain, for if it does, it is not faith, but
opinion. How, then, does it differ from
understanding? Even though faith is no
more uncertain than understanding, still it
is wrapped in mystery which understanding
is not. Finally, what you have understood
is not something you can inquire further
about, for if it is, you have not understood
it. Now, we prefer to know nothing more
than that which we already know by faith.
Our happiness will lack nothing when that
which is already certain to us will be
equally evident.

WHAT WE OUGHT TO CONTEMPLATE
IN THE HEAVENLY SPIRITS

*Gal 4:26

IV. 7. With these things taken care of, let us now direct our consideration to that Jerusalem which is above, our mother,* and as much as is lawful, or rather to the degree that it is given to us, let us search the unsearchable carefully and watchfully by all the three ways mentioned above. Indeed, first of all we have ascertained through reading and we hold through faith that the citizens there are powerful spirits, glorious and blessed; they are distinct persons, arranged in order of dignity, established from the beginning, in their order of rank, perfect in what they are, ethereal in body, endowed with immortality, not created impassible but made so, that is by grace, not by nature; pure of mind, with kind disposition, devoutly pious, wholly chaste, individual but unanimous, secure in peace, formed by God and dedicated to divine praise and service. All this we learn by reading, and we hold by faith. But as for their bodies, some are doubtful not only about their source, but whether they exist at all. Because of this if anyone thinks that this is more a matter of opinion, I do not dispute with him. Moreover, that they are endowed with understanding we hold not by faith, nor by opinion, but by understanding because they cannot be devoid of understanding and at the same time enjoy the possession of God. Likewise, certain names are known to us by hearing, through which

we can somehow detect and distinguish the
offices of the blessed ones, their merits, dignities and orders, even though the hearing of
mortal men does not perceive them clearly.
But that which does not come from hearing
does not come from faith, for 'faith comes
from hearing.'* Therefore, we say these
things as matters of opinion. Why have the
names of the heavenly beings been made
known if it is not even permitted, without
harm to our faith, to form some opinion
about the beings whose names they are?
These names are: Angels, Archangels, Virtues, Powers, Principalities, Dominions,
Thrones, Cherubim and Seraphim.[2] What do
these signify? Is there no difference between
those spirits who are simply called Angels
and those who are called Archangels?

8. What is the meaning of these different degrees? Let us suppose, unless you
can suggest something better, that they are
called Angels who are believed appointed
one to each man, and are sent to serve those
who are to obtain salvation, as Paul
teaches.* About these the Savior says,
'Their Angels continually behold the face
of the Father.'* Suppose that above these
are the Archangels who, as confidants of
the divine mysteries, are not sent except
for matters of extreme importance. We
read that one of these, the great Archangel
Gabriel, was sent to Mary, on a matter
which was, indeed, of the greatest importance.[3] Suppose that over these are the
Virtues by whose will or instigation signs
and wonders appear in the elements or are

Rom 10:17

Heb 1:14

Mt 18:10

constituted from the elements for the instruction of men. Perhaps this is why when you read in the Gospels, 'There will be signs in the sun, moon and stars,'* a little later you have, 'For the Virtues of heaven will be moved.'*[4] Without doubt, these are the spirits through whom powerful signs are accomplished. Let us suppose that superior to these are the Powers, by whose strength the power of darkness is checked and the malignity of this air is restrained so it cannot inflict what harm it might, so it cannot do evil unless it can be profitable to us. Suppose also that before these the Principalities are ranked, by whose moderation and wisdom all the principalities on earth are established, ruled, limited, transferred, diminished, and altered. Let us suppose that surpassing all these orders are the Dominions to whom the rest seem to be ministering spirits. Related to the Dominions, as to their masters, are the rule of the Principalities, the protection of the Powers, the operations of the Virtues, the revelations of the Archangels, and the provident care of the Angels. Let us suppose that the Thrones have ascended to recesses even higher than these, and that they are called Thrones because they are seated and they are seated because God is seated upon them. For he could not be seated upon those who are not seated. Do you ask what I judge this sitting to be? Supreme tranquility, most placid serenity, peace which surpasses all understanding.* Such is he, the Lord of

Lk 21:25

Lk 21:26

Phil 4:7

Sabbaoth, who sits upon the Throne, judging all things with tranquility; he is most placid, most serene, most peaceful. And he has established those as Thrones for himself which are most similar to him. Let us suppose the Cherubim drink from the very font of wisdom, the mouth of the Most High,* and pour forth a stream of knowledge to all the citizens of heaven. And see if it is not this which the Prophet speaks of: 'The stream of the river makes the city of God joyful.'* Let us suppose the Seraphim, spirits totally enkindled with divine fire, enkindle all so that each citizen is a lamp burning and shining:*[5] burning with love, shining with knowledge. *Ecclus 24:5

*Ps 45:5

*Jn 5:35

9. O Eugene, how good it is for us to be here!* But how much better it would be, if we could at sometime wholly follow where we have gone before in part. We have gone before in spirit, and not even our whole spirit, but only part, and too small a part. Our affections lie weighted down by this bodily mass, and cling to the mire with desires while only consideration, dry and delicate, flies before. And still with so little granted it as yet, it freely cries out, 'Lord I have loved the beauty of your house and the place where your glory dwells.'* What if the soul were totally recollected and with affections recalled from all the places they were held captive by fearing what should not be feared, loving what was unworthy, grieving vainly and more vainly rejoicing, it began to soar with total liberty, to drive on under the impulse of the spirit *Mt 17:4

*Ps 25:8

and to glide along in abundance of grace?
And when the soul has begun to move about
the illumined mansions and to examine
carefully even the bosom of Abraham, and
to look again upon the souls of martyrs
under the altar* (whatever that might be)[6]
dressed in their first robes* and patiently
awaiting their second, will it not say much
more insistently with the Prophet, 'One
thing I have asked of the Lord, this will I
seek, that I may dwell in the house of the
Lord all the days of my life, that I may see
the will of the Lord, and visit his tem-
ple'?*[7] Is not the heart of God to be seen
there? Is it not shown there what is the
good, the acceptable, the perfect will of
God:*[8] good in itself, pleasing in its
effects, acceptable to those enjoying it,
perfect to those who are perfect and who
seek nothing beyond it? His heart of
mercy lies open,* his thoughts of peace lie
revealed,† the riches of his salvation,*
the mysteries of his good will, the secrets
of his kindness, which are hidden from
mortals and beyond the comprehension of
even the elect. This, indeed, is for the good
of their salvation, so they do not cease
fearing before they are found suited for
loving worthily.

10. In these who are called Seraphim
we can perceive how he loves who has
nothing to elicit his love but who does not
hate anything which he has made;* we can
perceive how he supports those whom he
has made to be saved, how he carries them
forward, how he embraces them, how that

Rev 6:9
Lk 15:22

Ps 26:4

Rom 12:2

Lk 1:78
†Jer 29:11
Is 33:6

Wis 11:25

fire* consumes the youthful sins of the
elect and the chaff of their ignorance,
purging it and rendering it worthy of his
love. We can see in the Cherubim, who are
called the fullness of knowledge, that the
Lord is a God of knowledge* who alone is
ignorant of ignorance alone, who is totally
light and in whom there is no darkness,*
who is totally an eye which never fails
because it is never closed, who does not
seek a light outside himself toward which
he moves so he can see for he who sees is
himself the source of his sight. We can see
how he sits upon the Thrones as a judge
who causes no fear among the innocent
and who cannot be circumvented and does
not wish to circumvent, for he loves and he
sees as we have described above. And his
sitting does not lack meaning; it is a sign of
tranquility. Let my judgment, I pray,
come forth from such a countenance* in
which there is love and from which error
and disturbance are absent. In the Dominions we can see how great is the majesty
of the Lord at whose nod an empire is
established with boundaries that are universal and eternal. In the Principalities we
can see the principle from which all things
derive, and that just as a door hangs from a
hinge, so the universe depends on him as its
ruler. In the Powers it is seen how mightily
this same Prince protects those whom he
rules, repelling and driving off hostile
powers. In the Virtues we can see that
there is everywhere equally present one
noble force through which all things have

*Deut 4:24;
Heb 12:29

*1 Sam 2:3

*1 Jn 1;5

*Cf. Ps 16:2

their being, which is vivifying, efficacious, invisible and immobile yet beneficially moving all things and firmly sustaining them. When it appears among mortals with somewhat unusual effects, men call these effects miracles or prodigies. Finally we can see and admire in the Angels and Archangels the truth and the proof of that saying, 'For he cares about us.'* He does not cease to delight us with visits from such great beings, to instruct us by their revelations, to admonish us by their suggestions and to comfort us by their zeal.

*1 Pet 5:7

V. 11. All of this has been conferred on these spirits by him who created them, one and the same supreme Spirit distributing to each as he wills.* He achieves all this in them; he has given this to them to achieve, but in a different way. The Seraphim burn, but with the fire of God, or rather with the fire which is God. What is special with them is that they love, but not as much as God, nor in the same way. The Cherubim shine and are prominent by their knowledge, but this is through participation in the truth, and not as Truth itself or to the same degree as Truth. The Thrones are seated, but by the favor of the one sitting upon them. They judge with tranquility, but not in the measure or the manner of the peace bestowing peace, of that peace which surpasses all understanding.* The Dominions rule, but they rule under the Lord and likewise they serve him. What is this compared to his supreme, everlasting, and

*1 Cor 12:11

*Phil 4:7

singular dominion? The Principalities rule and govern, but they are also governed so that now they would not know how to govern if they should cease to be governed. The Powers excel in strength, but the one to whom they owe their strength is strong in a different way, and stronger than they, in fact, he is not so much strong as he is strength itself.

The Virtues in accordance with their ministry engage in arousing the sluggish hearts of men by a show of signs; but it is his virtue remaining in them which accomplishes what is done. They also bring about what is done, but in comparison with his virtue they do nothing. In fact, the difference is so great that the Prophet says as it were to him alone, 'You are God who do marvelous things.'* Again the same Prophet of him, 'Alone he does marvelous things.'* Angels and Archangels are present, but he is closer to us who is not only present but within us. *Ps 76:15 *Ps 135:4

12. But if you should say an Angel can be present within us, I do not deny it. I remember it is written, 'An Angel who spoke in me . . . .'* Nevertheless, there is a difference and it is this: the Angel is within a man suggesting the good, not effecting it; he is in us urging us toward the good, not creating it. God is present in a man in such a way that he causes an effect, so that he infuses or rather is infused and partaken of; this occurs in such a way that someone need not fear to say that God is one spirit with our spirit, even if he is not one person *Zech 1:14

or one substance with us. Indeed, you have the statement, 'Who adheres to God is one spirit with him.'* Therefore, the Angel is with the soul; God is in the soul. The Angel is in the soul as its companion, God as its life.

*1 Cor 6:17

Thus, just as the soul sees with its eyes, hears with its ears, smells with its nose, tastes with its mouth, touches with the rest of its body, so God accomplishes different ends through different spirits; for example, in some he shows himself loving, in others perceiving, in others, doing other things, just as the manifestation of the Spirit is given to each for his own good.* Who is this who is so common in our speech but in reality is so distant? How do we speak of him in our conversations when hidden in his majesty he completely avoids our sight and our affections? Hear what he says to men, 'As the heavens are higher than the earth, so are my ways higher than your ways and my thoughts than your thoughts.'* We are said to love, and so is God; we are said to know, and so is God; and many more things of this kind. But God loves as charity, he knows as truth, he sits in judgment as justice, he rules as majesty, he governs as a principle, he protects as salvation, he operates as strength, he reveals as light, he assists as piety. And all of this the Angels also do, and so do we, but in a far inferior manner; not indeed because of the good which we are but by the good in which we share.

*1 Cor 12:7

*Is 55:9

WHAT IS TO BE CONTEMPLATED
IN THE ESSENCE OF GOD
THE HERESY OF THOSE WHO SAY:
'GOD IS GOD IN HIS DIVINITY,
BUT THE DIVINITY ITSELF IS NOT GOD.'
GOD IS ONE.

VI. 13. Right now, pass over those spirits and perhaps you may be able to say with the bride, 'Scarcely had I passed them and I found him whom my soul loves.'* Who is he? Clearly no better answer occurs to me than, 'He who is.'* He wished this to be answered of him; he taught this to Moses and urged him to say to the people, 'He who is has sent me to you.'* Indeed, this is fitting; nothing is more appropriate for the eternity which God is. If you should say of God anything good, or great, or blessed, or wise, or any such thing, it is summed up in this phrase which says, 'He is.' For his being is what all these things are. If you should add a hundred such attributes, you would not go beyond his essence. If you should say these things you would add nothing; if you should not say them, you would take nothing away. If you have already perceived how singular, how supreme his being is, do you not judge that by comparison whatever God is not, is non-being rather than being? Again, what is God? That without which nothing exists.* Just as nothing can exist without him, so he cannot exist without himself: he exists for himself, he exists for all, and consequently in some way he alone exists who is his own

*Song 3:4

*Ex 3:14

*Ibid.

*Jn 1:3

Jn 8:25

existence and that of all else. What is God? The Beginning; this is the answer he gave of himself.* Many things in the world are spoken of as beginnings, and this is in respect to what comes after them. Yet if you look back and see something which precedes another, you will call that the beginning. Therefore, if you seek the true and absolute beginning, you must discover that which has no beginning. That from which everything began clearly had no beginning itself, for if it began, it must have begun from some source. For nothing begins from itself, unless someone thinks that something which does not exist can cause itself to be or that something existed before it came to be, but since reason approves of neither of these it is clear that nothing exists as its own beginning. Moreover, what had its beginning from another was not first. Therefore, the true beginning in no way had a beginning, but totally began from itself.

14. What is God? A being for whom the ages have neither approached nor departed, and yet are not coeternal. What is God? 'From whom and through whom and in whom are all things.'* From whom are all things through creation, not as from a source; through whom are all things, lest you think there is one who is the author and one who is the maker; in whom are all things, not as in a place but as in power. From which are all things as if from one beginning; the author of all; through whom are all things, lest we think the maker a

Rom 11:36

second beginning; in whom are all things,
lest a third reality be introduced, that of
place. From whom are all things, not of
whom, because God is not matter; he is
the efficient not the material cause. In
vain do philosophers seek the material:
God had no need of matter. He did not
seek a workshop or a craftsman. He made
everything through himself, in himself. Out
of what? Out of nothing; for if he made it
from something, he did not make that and
consequently did not make everything. Do
not suppose that from his own uncor-
rupted and incorruptible substance he made
so many things, for even if they are good,
they are corruptible.

Do you ask: if all things are in him,
where is he? I can answer nothing more
inadequately than this. What place can
contain him? Do you ask where he is not?
I cannot even answer that. What place is
without God? God is incomprehensible,*   *Jer 32:19*
but you have learned a great deal if you
discovered this about him: that he is nowhere who is not enclosed in a place,
and he is everywhere who is not excluded
from a place. In his own sublime and
incomprehensible way, just as all things
are in him,* so he is in all things.† For, as   *Col 1:16–17*
the Evangelist says, 'He was in the world.'*   †1 Cor 15:28
Furthermore, we know that where he was   *Jn 1:10*
before the world was made, there he is
today. There is no need to ask further
where he was: nothing existed except him,
therefore he was in himself.

VII. 15. What is God? That than which nothing better can be thought.[9] If you accept this, you should not assert that there is anything from which God has his existence, and which God is not. That without a doubt would be better than God. How can it not be better than God, if it is not God and yet causes God to be? But it is better for us to confess that the divinity by which God is said to exist is not distinct from God. There is nothing in God but God. 'What?' they say, 'Do you deny that God exists through his divinity?' No, but he does not exist by anything other than what he is. If you have found something else, may the Triune God help me, I will rise up most firmly against it. Quaternity sets limits to the earth; it is not a characteristic of the Deity.[10] God is Trinity, God is each of three persons. If it pleases you to add a fourth divinity, I am already convinced that what is not God should not be worshipped. I think you agree, for 'You shall worship the Lord your God and him only shall you serve.'*

*Lk 4:8

It is a glorious divinity which does not dare claim for itself divine honor! But it is better that we reject this fourth element entirely, than receive it without honor. Many things are said to be in God, and surely this is a true and Catholic statement, but the many are one. Otherwise, if we were to think them separate, we have not a four-fold divinity, but a hundred-fold. For example, we say God is great, good, just, and innumerable other such things, but

unless you consider all as one in God and
with God, you will have a multiple God.

16. But I am not unable to conceive of
a better God than this one of yours. Do
you ask what he is? Pure simplicity. True
judgment prefers a simple nature to a multiple one. I know what the usual response
is to this; they claim, 'We do not attribute
many things to God in order for him to
exist, but only one—divinity.' You assert,
therefore, a dual God, if not a multiple
God, and you have not achieved pure
simplicity nor attained that than which
nothing better can be thought. That is not
simple which is subject to even one form
just as she is not a virgin who has known
even one man. I can say confidently that
even he who is only double will not be my
God. For I have a better one. I grant that I
prefer this one to a manifold, multiple
one, but clearly I reject him for a simple
God. My God is universal.[11] He does not
possess this or that attribute anymore than
he possesses these or those. He is who he
is,* not what he is. Pure, simple, whole,   *Ex 3:14*
perfect, constant, in no way temporal or
local, taking nothing of the material world
into himself, divesting nothing of himself
on it, he possesses nothing which can be
divided into numbers, nothing which can
be gathered into a unit. Indeed, he is one,
but not a composite. He does not consist
of parts like the body; he is not distended
in affections like the soul; he is not subject
to forms as everything which has been
made,[12] nor to a single form as it seems to

some of our contemporaries.[13] Great praise for God—that he claims to be preserved from formlessness by a single form, which is to say that everything else is indebted to many forms for what it is, but God is indebted to only one! What is this? Shall he, by whose beneficence things exist owe existence to another benefactor? That praise, as the saying goes, is tantamount to blasphemy. Is it not greater to be in need of nothing than of one thing? Revere God enough to attribute the greater to him. If your heart could ascend to this level, how will you place your God lower? He is his own form, he is his own essence. For the meantime, I look up to him at this level and if another higher level should appear I will grant him that instead. Must we fear that thought will surpass him? However lofty a height it might attain, he is beyond it. It is absurd to seek the Most High beneath the heights to which man's thoughts can attain; to place God there is impious. He must be sought beyond the limits of our thought and not within them.

17.   Ascend to a still loftier heart, if you can, and God will be exalted.* God is not formed, he is form. God is not affected, he is affection. God is not a composite, he is pure and simple. And so you may clearly know what I mean by simple: it is the same as one. God is as simple as he is one. But he is one as nothing else is. If it could be said, he is one to the superlative degree.[14] The sun is one for there is no other; the moon is one because likewise

there is no other. And God is one in the
same way, but more so. What is this more?
He is the one even with respect to himself.
Do you wish this to be explained to you?
He is always the same, and in a single way.
The sun is not one in this way, nor is the
moon. Each declares that it is not one, the
sun by its movements, the moon by its
phases. God, however, is not only one with
respect to himself, he is also one in himself.
He has nothing in him but himself. He
undergoes no change with the passage of
time, nor any alteration in his substance.
Hence Boethius says of God, 'This is
truly one in which there is no number
in which there is nothing beyond that
which it is. Neither can it be made
subject to forms, for it is form.'* Compare   *Boethius,
to this one everything that can be called   De trinitate 2,
one and the latter will not be one. But   PL 64:1250C
God is Trinity. What then? Do we destroy
what has been said about unity because we
introduce trinity? No, but we establish
what the unity is. We say Father, we say
Son, we say Holy Spirit, but we speak not
of three Gods, but one.[15] What is the
meaning of this number without number, if
I may use such an expression? If there are
three, how is there not number? If one,
where is number? You say, 'But I have
something which I can number and something I cannot: the substance is one, the
persons are three. What is marvelous, or
what is obscure in this?' 'Nothing, if the
persons are thought of separate from the
substance. But now since the three persons

are the substance, and the one substance
the three persons, who can deny there is
number here? Truly they are three. But
who can number them? For truly they are
one. If you think this an easy explanation,
tell me what you have enumerated when
you speak of three. Natures? There is one.
Essences? There is one. Substances? There
is one. Deities? There is one. You say, 'I
number not these but the persons.' 'And
they are not that one nature, that one
essence, that one substance, that one divinity? You are Catholic, you will hardly
grant this.'

THE UNITY OF THE TRINITY

VIII. 18. The Catholic faith confesses
that the properties of the persons are iden-
tical with the one God, the one divine substance, the one divine nature, the one
supreme, divine majesty. Therefore, count,
if you can, the persons without the substance which they are, or the properties
without the persons which they are. But if
someone should try to separate either the
persons from the substance or the properties from the persons, I do not know
how he could say that he worships the
Trinity, after having exceeded it with such
a multiplicity of elements. Therefore, let
us speak of three but without prejudice to
unity; let us speak of one, but not to the
confusion of Trinity. For these are not
empty names nor words signifying nothing.

Does anyone ask how this is possible? Let it suffice for him to believe this, not as something evident from reason, nor wavering with opinion, but as something certified by faith. This is a great mystery, to be worshipped, not investigated. How can plurality exist in unity and in such a unity, and this unity in plurality? To scrutinize this is temerity; to believe it is piety; to know it is life, even eternal life.* Wherefore, Eugene, if you think it worthwhile, consider now many kinds of 'one,' so that the pre-eminence of this singular 'one' may become more evident. There is a unity which can be called collective, when, for example, many stones make one pile. There is a constituted unity where many members make up one body or many parts make some kind of whole. There is also conjugal unity by which two are no longer two, but one flesh. There is natural unity whereby soul and flesh give birth to one man. There is moral unity by which the man of virtue strives to be free of instability and inconsistency and to be always one with himself. There is the unity of accord when through charity among many men there is one heart and one soul. There is also the unity of desire when the soul, clinging to God with all its desires, is one spirit with him.* And there is the unity of condescension whereby our clay was assumed by the Word of God into a single person.

    19. But what are all of these compared to that supreme and, if I may use the phrase, unique unity, when consubstan-

*Cf. Jn 17:3

*1 Cor 6:17

tiality effects the unit? Whichever of those you liken to this unity will be in some way one, but there is no comparison between them. Therefore, among everything which can rightly be called one, the first place is held by the unity of the Trinity which is three persons in one substance. It excels the second place where conversely three substances are one person in Christ. Moreover, this and whatever else can be spoken of as one is called one in imitation of that supreme unity, not by comparison with it, as true and prudent consideration proves. We do not depart from this profession of unity by the assertion of three, since in this Trinity we do not acknowledge multiplicity, just as in the unity we acknowledge no solitude. And, therefore, when I say 'one,' the number of the Trinity does not disturb me, for it does not increase the essence, does not change it, does not divide it. Likewise, when I say 'three,' the concept of unity does not censure me, for this unity does not confuse the three entities or three beings, nor reduce them to singularity.

THE UNITY OF SOUL AND BODY

IX. 20. I confess I feel the same also about that unity to which I have assigned a place of honor second to that of the Trinity among all other unities. I say that in Christ, the Word, a soul and flesh are one person without confusion of essences, and that without prejudice to the unity of his person, they remain numerically distinct. And I would not deny that this unity belongs to that kind of unity by which the soul and the flesh are one man.[16] It was fitting, indeed, that the mystery which was accomplished on man's behalf should be in close and intimate harmony with the nature of man. It was also fitting that it conform to that supreme unity which is in God and is God, so that just as in God three persons are one essence, so here by a most appropriate turn-about three essences are one person. Do you see how beautifully between either unit is placed this unity in him who has been appointed mediator of God and man, the man Christ Jesus?* It is beautifully appropriate, I say, in that the mystery of salvation corresponds by suitable degree of similarity both to the Savior and to the saved. Thus this unity stands at the middle between the two unities, yielding to the one, pre-eminent over the other, as much less than the greater as greater than the lesser.

    *1 Tim 2:5

21. The person Christ in whom God and man are one manifests in himself[17] such a great and powerful expression of unity that you would not err if you should predicate these two of one another, that is, announcing truly and in accord with Catholic faith that God is man and man God. You may not similarly, however, except most absurdly, predicate either flesh of the soul, or soul of flesh, even though similarly soul and flesh are one man. It is

*Rom 1:4

no surprise that the soul is not equally able by its vital intention (though this is quite strong) to join flesh to itself, and by its affections to bind it to itself, as divinity has done with that man who was predestined the son of God in power.* Divine predestination is a long and powerful chain for binding, for it reaches from eternity. What is longer than eternity? What is stronger than divinity? Hence it is that this unity cannot be dissolved even by death, although the body and the soul are separated from one another. And perhaps he sensed this who declared himself unworthy to loose the strap of his sandal.*

*Mk 1:7:
St John the
Baptist

THREE MEASURES OF
LEAVENED FLOUR IN A LOAF

*Mt 13:3,
Lk 13:21

X. 22. It would not seem incongruous to me if someone were to say that the three measures of flour in the Gospel,* which when mixed and leavened formed one loaf of bread, have some relevance to these three essences in Christ. How well the Woman leavened them so that not even with the division of body and soul was the Word separated from the body or the soul! The inseparable unity remained even in the separation. For, the partial separation which occurred could not alter the unity in all three. Whether the two were joined or separated, nonetheless, the unity of the person endured in the three. The Word, the soul and the body even after death

remained one and the same Christ, one and
the same person. I feel that this mixture
and leavening was brought about in the
womb of the Virgin and this Woman herself did the mixing and the leavening; for I
may say, perhaps not without reason, that
the leaven was Mary's faith. She is truly
blessed who believed, because what was
spoken to her by the Lord was accom-
plished in her.* But these things would not   *Lk 1:45
have been accomplished unless, as the Lord
said,* all were leavened and leavened per-   *Mt 13:33
petually, maintaining for us as much in
death as in life the one, perfect mediator
of God and men with his divinity, the man
Christ Jesus.*   *1 Tim 2:5

CONCERNING THOSE WHO ASSERT
THE FLESH OF CHRIST
IS SOMETHING NEW CREATED IN THE VIRGIN
AND NOT TAKEN FROM
THE FLESH OF THE VIRGIN

23. Notice in this wonderful mystery the
marvelous and appropriate degrees of distinction, equal in number to the measures
of flour: the new, the old, the eternal. The
new is the soul, believed created from nothing at the moment it was infused; the old
is the flesh, known to have been passed on
from the very first man, that is, from Adam.
The eternal is the Word, asserted with un-
doubtable truth to be coeternal from the
eternal Father and begotten of him. There is
in these three, if you observe carefully, a

triple kind of divine power in that something has been made from nothing, something new has been made from something old, and something eternal and blessed from something damned and dead. What has this to do with our salvation? Much in every way: first of all, because brought to nothing by sin, we are in some way created anew by this so that we are somehow the beginning of his creation;* second, because we have been transferred from the old servitude to the freedom of the sons of God* and we walk in the newness of spirit;* finally, because we have been called from the power of darkness* to the kingdom of eternal brightness in which even now he has caused us to sit in Christ.* Let them be cut off from us who try to cut us off from the flesh of Christ, impiously asserting that it was created new in the Virgin and not taken from the Virgin. Long ago, the prophetic spirit beautifully dealt with this statement, rather this blasphemy of godless men, when it said, 'A shoot shall come forth from the root of Jesse, and a flower spring up from his root.'* It could have said, 'and a flower from the shoot,' but it preferred 'from the root,' so as to show that the flower and the shoot had the same origin. Therefore, flesh was assumed from the source from which the Virgin came forth and was not created new in the Virgin for it came from the same root.

*Jas 1:18

*Rom 8:21
*Rom 6:4; 7:6
*Col 1:13

*Eph 2:6

*Is 11:1

THE MANY EXPRESSIONS
OF DIVINE CONTEMPLATION

XI. 24. Perhaps you will be somewhat vexed if we continue to ask what God is, both because this has been asked so often already and because you doubt the answer can be found? I tell you, Father Eugene, it is God alone who can never be sought in vain,* even when he cannot be found. *Cf. Is 45:19* Your experience may teach you this, but if not, believe an expert, not me, but the Holy One who said, 'Lord, you are good to those who hope in you, to the soul who seeks you.'* Therefore, what is God? He is *Lam 3:25* that which is to the universe, the end; to the elect, salvation; to himself, he alone knows. What is God? Omnipotent will, benevolent virtue, eternal light, unchangeable reason, supreme blessedness; he creates souls to share in himself, vivifies them that they may experience him, causes them to desire him, enlarges them to receive him, justifies them that they may merit him; he inflames them with zeal, brings them to fruition, leads them in justice, molds them in benevolence, directs them in wisdom, strengthens them in virtue, visits them in consolation, enlightens them with knowledge, preserves them to immortality, fills them with happiness, surrounds them with security.

GOD IS NO LESS THE PUNISHMENT
OF THE PERVERSE
THAN THE GLORY OF THE HUMBLE

XII. 25. What is God? No less the punishment of the perverse than the glory of the humble; for he is, so to speak, the spiritual principle of equity, unalterable and uncompromising, indeed, pervading everywhere, and every evil that comes in contact with this principle must necessarily be confounded. And why should everything inflated or distorted not dash against such a principle and be shattered? Woe to anything which might be struck by a righteousness which knows not how to yield since it is also fortitude. What is so contrary and adverse to an evil will than always to strive, always to clash, but in vain? Woe to rebellious wills who reap only punishment for their opposition. What is so punishing as always to will what will never be and always to oppose what will always be. What is so condemned as a will given over to this compulsion to desire and aversion so it no longer experiences either except perversely and, therefore, wretchedly. Never will it obtain what it wishes, and what it does not wish it will nonetheless endure forever. It is completely just that he who is never attracted to what is right should never attain what pleases him. Who arranges this? The righteous Lord our God, *Ps 91:16; 17:27* who deals perversely with the perverse.* Never do right and wrong agree, for they are adverse to one another even though

they do not harm one another. Harm is
done to the other, certainly not to God!
'It is hard for you,' he says, 'to kick
against the goad.'* That is, it is not hard   *Acts 9:5*
for the goad, but for the kicker. God is also
the punishment of base man, for he is
light. And what is as hateful to obscene,
profligate minds? Truly, 'everyone who
does evil hates the light.'* But I say, can   *Jn 3:20*
they not avoid it? Not at all. It shines
in the darkness and the darkness does not
comprehend it.'* The light sees the dark-   *Jn 1:5*
ness because for it to shine is to see; but
the light in turn is not seen by the darkness
for the darkness does not comprehend it.*   *Ibid.*
It is seen so it can be confounded; it does
not see lest it be consoled. It is seen not
only by the light, but in the light. By
whom? By everyone who sees, so that the
multitude of witnesses might heighten their
confusion. But out of such a large number
of spectators no eye is more troublesome
to each than his own. There is no scrutiny,
either in heaven or on earth which a
clouded conscience would like to escape
more nor any which it is less able to. The
darkness does not hide even itself: they see
themselves who see nothing else. The works
of darkness follow them and there is no
place where they can hide themselves from
them, not even in darkness. This is the
worm which does not die:* the memory of   *Mk 9:43*
things past.* Once it is inserted, or rather   *Wis 11:13*
is born in a person through sin, it clings
there stubbornly, never after to be removed. It does not stop gnawing at the

conscience; and, feeding on this truly inexhaustible food, it perpetuates its life, I shudder at this gnawing worm and such a living death. I shudder to fall into the hands of this living death, this dying life.

26. Such is the second death* which never annihilates but always kills. Who can grant that they die once and not die forever? Those who say to the mountains, 'Fall upon us,' and to the hills, 'cover us,'* what do they want but to end death or avoid it through the kindness of death? Indeed, it is said, 'They will call upon death but death will not come.'* Look at this more closely. It is agreed that the soul is immortal and that it will never exist without its memory, or else it would no longer be the soul. Therefore, while the soul exists the memory endures. But in what state? Defiled with shameful acts, horrid with crimes, puffed up with vanity, befouled and neglected. What used to be has passed away but it has not passed away: it has passed out of reach but not out of mind. What has been done cannot be undone. Thus, although the doing occurred at a definite time, the having done remains for eternity. That does not pass with time which passes through time. Therefore, a wrong you have done and remember for eternity must of necessity torment you for eternity. Thus you will experience the truth of the statement, 'I will stand before you and accuse you.'* The Lord has spoken and everyone who is opposed to him must also be opposed to himself so that he

*Rev 20:14

*Lk 23:30

*Job 3:21

*Ps 49:21

finally complains, 'O guardian of men, why have you set me opposed to you, why have I become a burden to myself?'* Thus it is, Eugene. No being can be opposed to God and be in harmony with itself; whoever is accused by God is likewise accused by himself. There will surely be no way in the next life that reason can ignore truth or that the soul, stripped of the bodily members and gathered into itself, can avoid the gaze of reason. How could this happen, when death has stunned and imprisoned the senses through which the soul used to go out eagerly and depart from itself into the transient beauty of this world. Do you see that nothing is lacking for the confusion of base men when they will be brought forth to become a spectacle to God, the angels, and to men themselves?* O how badly all the evil have been disposed, indeed they are set in opposition to this torment of unyielding justice, and exposed to the light of naked truth. Is this not to be buffeted perpetually and perpetually confounded? The prophet says, 'Destroy them with a double destruction, O Lord, our God.'*

*Job 7:20

*1 Cor 4:9

*Jer 17:18

WHAT IS THE LENGTH, THE WIDTH, THE HEIGHT AND THE DEPTH

XIII. 27. What is God? The length, the width, the height and the depth.* You say, 'What do you hold yourself up as a teacher of quaternity, which you detested before? Not

*Eph 3:18

at all, I detested it, and I still detest it. I
seem to have mentioned many things, but
they are one. The one God has been described for our understanding, not as he actually is. Divisions exist in our understanding, not in God. There are various names,
many paths; but one thing is signified by the
names, one is sought by the paths. Divisions
of substance are not intended by this quaternity, nor dimensions such as we observe
in bodies; nor distinction of person such as
we adore in the Trinity; nor number of
properties such as we confess are present
in the persons themselves, even if they are
not distinct from the persons. In other
words, in God one of these is what the
four are; the four are what one is. But we
cannot deal with the simplicity of God;
while we strive to comprehend him as one,
he appears to us as fourfold. This is caused

1 Cor 13:12   by our vision through a glass darkly,* the
only way we can see in this life. But when
we see him face to face we will see him as

Ibid; 1 Jn 3:2   he is.* At that time the fragile gaze of our
souls, however assiduously applied, will in
no way return or break down into its own
multiplicity. It will draw more together,
unite, and conform itself to God's unity,
or rather to God who is unity, so one will
answer the other face to face. Indeed, 'we
will be like him because we will see him as

1 Jn 3:2   he is.'* A blessed vision for which he
rightly sighed who said, 'My face has

Ps 26:8   sought you, your face, Lord, do I seek.'*
And because the search is yet going on, let
us climb into the four-horse chariot, since

we are still weak and feeble and we need
such a vehicle, if even in this way we can
apprehend him by whom we are appre-
hended,* for he is the reason for this vehi-   *Phil 3:12
cle. Now, we have this instruction from the
charioteer and him who first showed us this
chariot, that we should strive 'to comprehend with all the saints what is the length,
the width, the height, and the depth.'* He   *Eph 3:18
says, 'to comprehend' not 'to know,' so that
not content with a curiosity for knowledge
we should long for fruition with all our care.
Fruition is not in knowledge, but in comprehension. Indeed, as someone says, 'It is a
sin for him who knows what is good and
does not do it.'* And Paul in another place   *Jas 4:17
says, 'Thus run so you may comprehend.'*   *1 Cor 9:24
I will explain below what comprehension is.

28.   Therefore, what is God? 'Length,' I
say. What is that? Eternity. This is so long
that it has no end, either in space or in time.
He is also width. And what is that? Charity.
And by what boundaries is this charity con-
fined in God who hates none of the things
he has made?* Indeed, 'he causes his sun to   *Wis 11:25
rise upon the good and the evil, and rain
falls upon the just and the unjust.'* There-   *Mt 5:45
fore his bosom encloses even his enemies.
And not even content with this, he stretches
to infinity, exceeding not only every affection, but every thought, as the Apostle goes
on to say, 'and to know the charity of Christ
which surpasses all understanding.'* What   *Eph 3:19
more can I say? It is eternal; unless this is
perhaps greater: it is eternity. Do you see that
the width is as great as the length? Would

that you could see not just how great it is, but that you could see it itself: that one is what the other is; that one is no less than two, that two are no more than one. God is eternity, God is charity:* length without extension, width without distension. In both he exceeds the limits of space and time, but by the freedom of his nature, not by the enormity of his substance. In such a way he is without measure who has made all things in measure;* and although he is without measure, this is the measure of his immensity.

29. Again, what is God? The height and depth.* By the one he is above all, by the other he is below all. It is evident that in the deity equity is nowhere defective, that it stands firm on every side, that it is immutably consistent. Consider his power as high and his wisdom as deep. These correspond equally with one another: his height is known to be unattainable, and his depth to be equally inscrutable. Paul marvels at this and says, 'O the depth of the riches of the knowledge and wisdom of God, how inscrutable are his judgments and how unsearchable his way!'* Freely we exclaim with Paul, looking upon the most simple unity of these attributes in God and with God: O powerful wisdom, reaching everywhere mightily!* O wise power, disposing all things sweetly!† One reality, multiple effects and various operations. And that one reality is length because of eternity, width because of charity, height because of majesty, depth because of wisdom.

*1 Jn 4:16

*Wis 11:21

*Eph 3:18

*Rom 11:33

*Wis 8:1
†Ibid.

XIV. 30. We know these things. Do we
think, therefore, we have also comprehended them? It is not disputation but
sanctity that comprehends them, if, however, what is incomprehensible can in any
way be comprehended. But unless it could,
the Apostle would not have said what we
should comprehend with all the saints.*   *Eph 3:18
The saints, then, comprehend. Do you ask
how? If you are a saint, you have comprehended and you know; if you are not, be
one and you will know through your own
experience. Holy affection makes a saint,
and this affection is two-fold: holy fear of
the Lord and holy love. The soul affected
perfectly by these comprehends as with
two arms, and embraces, binds and holds,
and says, 'I held him and I will not let him
go.'* Indeed, fear corresponds to height   *Song 3:4
and depth; love to width and length. What
is so to be feared as power which you
cannot resist, as wisdom from which you
cannot hide? God could be feared less if
he were lacking either of these. As it is, it is
perfectly fitting that you fear him for he is
not without an eye which sees all, nor a
hand which is all-powerful. What, moreover, is so loveable as love itself, by which
you love and by which you are loved? Still,
it is made more loveable by its union with
eternity for it dispels suspicion since it
does not die. Therefore, love with perseverance and patience and you have
length; widen your love to include your
enemies and you possess width; also, be
God-fearing and observant in everything

you do and you have obtained height
and depth.

31.   Or, if you prefer, four attributes of
yours correspond to the four divine attributes. You bring this about if you marvel,
if you fear, if you are fervent, if you
persevere. Clearly, the loftiness of majesty
must be marveled at; the abyss of God's
judgments must be feared. Charity demands
fervor; eternity requires perseverance and
endurance. Who marvels if not he who
contemplates the glory of God? Who fears
if not he who examines the depths of
wisdom? Who is fervent if not he who meditates on the charity of God? Who endures
and perseveres in love if not he who
emulates the eternity of charity? Indeed,
perseverance offers a certain image of
eternity, for it is to perseverance alone that
eternity is given, or rather it is perseverance
alone that gives man to eternity, as the
Lord says, 'He who perseveres to the end
Mt 10:22   shall be saved.'

32.   And now, observe that in these four
are four kinds of contemplation. The first
and greatest contemplation is the admira-
tion of majesty. This requires a purified
heart so that, freed from vices and released
from sin, it can easily rise to heavenly
things, and sometimes this contemplation
holds the onlooker suspended in astonish-
ment and ecstasy, if only for a brief
moment. A second kind of contemplation
is necessary for him: it consists in observing
the judgments of God. While this contemplation greatly disturbs the onlooker by

its fearful aspect it drives out vices, establishes virtues, initiates into wisdom, preserves humility. Indeed, humility is the true and firm foundation of the virtues. For, if humility should waver, the system of virtues is ruined. The third contemplation is occupied with, or rather takes leisure in, the remembrance of blessings and, lest it abandon a person as ungrateful, it urges the rememberer toward love for his Benefactor. Of such the Prophet speaks, saying to the Lord, 'They shall declare the memory of the abundance of your sweetness.'* The fourth contemplation, which *Ps 144:7* forgets what is behind, rests in the sole expectation of what has been promised, and this, since it is the meditation of eternity—for what is promised is eternal—nourishes patience and gives vigor to perseverance. I think it is easy now to compare our four terms with those of the Apostle: for meditation on the promises encompasses length; remembrance of blessing encompasses width; contemplation of majesty, height; examination of judgments, depth. He must still be sought who has not yet sufficiently been found and who cannot be sought too much; but he is perhaps more worthily sought and more easily found by prayer than by discussion. Therefore, let this be the end of the book but not the end of the search.

THE END

FIVE BOOKS ON CONSIDERATION
ADVICE TO A POPE

APPENDICES

APPENDICES

The five books of *De consideratione ad Eugenium Papam* were addressed to Pope Eugene III (February 15, 1145 – July 8, 1153). Eugene, of the family of Paganelli at Montemagno, and vidame of the church of Pisa,[1] entered Clairvaux in 1138; in 1139 he was sent to establish a Cistercian monastery in Italy; after a brief stay at the Saint Sylvester near Farfa, he proceeded, on the order of Innocent II, to that of Saints Vincent and Anastasius *ad aquas Salvias.* When Pope Lucius II died in the siege of the Capitol which the Senate had occupied, Eugene III was elected, in the church of Saint Cesarius, to succeed him. Rather than recognize the encroachments of the Romans, Eugene preferred to retire to the monastery of Farfa, north of Rome. There he was consecrated on February 18.[2] In a letter addressed to the cardinals after the election, Saint Bernard spoke of the new Pope: 'I am not at ease, because he is a delicate son and his sensitive timidity is more accustomed to retirement than to treat of external affairs. One can rightly fear that he will not fulfill his apostolic task with all the authority he ought.'[3]

As soon as he learned of the election of Eugene III, Saint Bernard sent his former disciple a letter[4] which is almost a sketch of the *De consideratione:* The pope is the friend of the Spouse and must not say, in speaking of the Church, 'My Princess,' but 'The Princess.' He must act with a spirit of service and not of domination, knowing that honors can cloud the mind. He must imitate Saint Peter who said: 'I have neither gold nor silver.' And, Saint Bernard adds: 'Who shall grant to me that before I die I could see the Church of God as it was in antiquity when the Apostles cast their nets to fish not for silver or for gold but for souls?'[5] The pope, in the midst of his apostolic duties, ought not to forget that he is a man.[6]

DATE OF COMPOSITION

In 1149 *De consideratione* was already sufficiently advanced so that Nicholas of Clairvaux, the secretary of Saint Bernard, could announce the dispatch of Book One to Peter the Venerable.[1] Book Two was begun after the failure of the Second Crusade (July, 1148). At the beginning of this book[2] a passage is devoted to this disaster. Book Three was written shortly after the death of Bishop Hugh of Mâcon in 1152 for Saint Bernard speaks of the recent choice of a successor to Hugh. As Bernard indicates, this took place four years after the commencement of the Council of Reims (March 21, 1148).[3] Book Five was completed in 1152–1153. Geoffrey of Auxerre[4] informs us that Saint Bernard continued to write even while on his deathbed.[5]

MANUSCRIPTS

The seventy oldest manuscripts of the treatise, *On Consideration,* are distributed in three principal stems.[1]

A first group, whose archetype has not been found, is composed of manuscripts from the monasteries of Bavaria and of Austria which were dependent on the Abbey of Morimond.

The manuscripts of the second group are those found especially in England. They offer an ameliorated text, corrected, it seems, by Saint Bernard himself.

A third group of manuscripts provides a text intermediary between that of Morimond and that of England.

The Clairvaux recension, which has affinities with that of Morimond, is defective and has been further weakened by the errors of copyists and by the work of correctors.

SOURCES

Sacred Scripture

Like all the works of Saint Bernard, *On Consideration* is immersed in Sacred Scripture. Three books are most frequently cited: the Gospel of Saint John, the First Epistle to the Corinthians, and the Gospel of Saint Matthew. The Gospel of Saint Mark is only rarely used. The other books of more frequent use are the Epistle to the Romans, the Prophecies of Isaiah, the Second Letter to the Corinthians, Genesis, the Letter to the Ephesians, and the Book of Job. This last is a book often familiar to men whose health is precarious. The Books of Kings are especially used in Book Four, that of Judges in Book Two. The prophet Ezekiel is principally cited in Books Two and Four.

The Fathers of the Church

Saint Bernard did not invent the quadripartite division of the *De consideratione: te, sub te, circa te* and *supra te.*[1] It is found in Saint Augustine: 'Although what is to be loved falls into four categories: 1) what is above us, 2) what we are, 3) what is about us, and 4) what is below us, in regard to the second and fourth no precept had to be given.'[2]

One finds it also in the *De clericorum institutione*[3] of Rhabanus Maurus, which was written in 819, and in the *De fide spe et charitate*[4] of Paschasius Radbertus, composed forty-six years later. Dom Jean Leclercq has shown that the theme recurs very often in the authors of the twelfth century; Raoul Ardent, Eadmer, Hugh of Saint Victor, Peter Lombard, Hildebert of Lavardin, Gandolph of Bologna, Peter of Poitiers and Isaac of Stella all use it.[5] The immediate source of this schema in the *De considera-tione,* however, is thought by Father Leclercq to have been a ninth-century commentator on the Rule of Saint Bene-dict, Hildemar. In fact, Hildemar not only invites one to go from self to creatures to God[6] as Saint Bernard does in Books Two and Five, but he also suggests a distinction which one finds in Book Two: 'He ought to remember what he is. What he is, that he is a man; what he is, that he is a prelate.'[7] Even the term *consideratio* recurs with insistence in Hildemar.[8]

In Book Five we find a citation from the *De Trinitate* of Boethius[9] and an image of the chariot which is perhaps a recollection from Paschasius Radbertus.[10]

De consideratione is not without analogy to the *Regulae pastoralis liber* of Saint Gregory the Great, who so strongly marked the medieval concept of the bishop.[11] The term *consideratio* itself, which in the monastic tradi-tion signifies contemplation,[12] appears in the *Regulae*[13] where Saint Gregory, like Saint Bernard, accents the perils to prelates from multiple occupations. What is more, in the *De consideratione,* Saint Bernard twice appeals to the authority of Saint Gregory the Great and, in particular, notes the need of contemplation.[14]

In Book Five of the *De consideratione,* Saint Bernard appears to be influenced by the *Proslogion* of Saint Anselm.[15]

The Authors of Antiquity

First of all, Saint Bernard cites the Aristotelian 'mean.'[16] Also, the influence of the *Republic, Phaedrus,* and *Phaedo* of Plato on the *De consideratione* seems to be indicated.[17] The close of the work, *'Proinde is sit finis libri, sed non finis quaerendi,'*[18] recalls the *'denique sit finis quaerendi'* of the *Satires* of Horace.[19] A citation from Ovid appears in Book Four: 'It is not always possible for the doctor to heal the sick.'[20] Terms borrowed from Roman legal vocabulary, *assertor, defensor, ordinator, magister, advocator, legum moderator, canonum dispensator, vicarius,* abound in the *De consideratione.*[21]

INFLUENCE

In the autumn of 1155, Gerhoh, Provost of the college of regular canons of Reichersberg in Bavaria, addressed a letter concerned with Christian doctrine to Eberhard of Reifenberg, Bishop of Bamberg (1145–1170). In it he cites the teaching of the *De consideratione* on the Incarnation.[1] John of Salisbury cites the *De consideratione* a number of times in his *Polycraticus.*[2] In particular he borrows the passage relative to Cardinal Martin Cibo (+1144).[3]

Sermon Twenty-two of Innocent III[4] was inspired by certain passages of the *De consideratione*[5] and his Second Sermon for the Consecration of Prelates[6] cites it verbatim.[7] The expression *deus Pharaonis* in the *De consideratione*[8] is found in another sermon of Innocent III[9] which, following Saint Bernard,[10] sees in the immensity of the sea a symbol of the universal extent of the power of Peter. Boniface VIII (1294–1304) bases the formulas of his Bull *Unam Sanctam* on those of the *De consideratione.*[11] Dante knew this work of Saint Bernard,[12] which he seems to have read between 1308 and 1313.[13] The doctrine of his *De monarchia* with regard to the two swords[14] was inspired by that expounded in the *De consideratione.*[15] John of Paris, Marsilius of Padua, William of Ockham, Augustine Trionfo, Giles of Rome, William Durant and

Petrarch knew and cited the *De consideratione*. The theme of the 'lament of the Church,' so frequent in the fourteenth and fifteenth centuries, is suggested in the last chapter of the *De consideratione*.[16]

During the period of the Great Schism, the works of Saint Bernard continued to be used. At the Council of Basel, copies of the *De consideratione* were read, copied and sold.[17] The Camaldolese, A. Traversari (+1439) sent a copy of it to Eugene IV and recommended that he read it.[18] The cardinals and the pope of the fifteenth century had copies made of this work; numerous examples have been preserved at the Vatican Library.[19] It appears also on the register of the loans of this library.[20] Nicholas V (1447–1453) thought so highly of the *De consideratione* that he had a magnificent copy of it made for himself.[21]

John Wyclif, isolating from their context all the criticisms directed against the Curia, made use of these arguments against the papacy.[22] Erasmus also repeated the criticisms of the *De consideratione* against the Roman court, accused of lacking an evangelical spirit.[23] 'Dans ce livre,' wrote Calvin, 'c'est la vérité même qui parle par la bouche de saint Bernard.'[24]

Saint Ignatius repeated the fourfold distinction of reforming one's self, one's house, the court, and the city of Rome.[25] Anthony Carafa gave an edition of the *De consideratione* to Saint Pius V (1566–1572) who had it read during his meals and called it the *Decretum* of the popes. Gregory XIII (1572–1585) imitated him in this; Saint Charles Borromeo had given him a copy.[26] Urban VII (1885–1590) read it habitually and had it brought to the conclave where he was elected pope.[27]

Gregory XV (1621–1623) wished that all ecclesiastics, especially prelates, could have a pocket edition of it. French translations were multiplied in the seventeenth century: des Mares in 1658, Anthony of Saint Gabriel and Francis of Saint Claude in 1672. Pascal cites it in the

Provinciales.[28]   Bossuet   does   also   in   his   reply   to
Innocent XI.[29]

In the *Journal de l'âme* John XXIII wrote:

> I have some pages of the *De consideratione* of
> Saint Bernard read to me. . . . Nothing is more
> useful for a poor Pope like myself, and for a
> pope at any time. Something of that which did
> not redound to the honor of the clergy of Rome
> in the twelfth century remains forever. Thus, it
> is necessary to keep watch, to correct, and
> to endure.[30]

In the discourse of September 21, 1963, announcing the
reform of the Curia, Paul VI declared: 'Today, happily,
Saint Bernard . . . could no longer write the burning pages
which he did concerning the ecclesiastical world of Rome.'

The *De consideratione* proposed to a pope of the
twelfth century a positive program of simplicity, of
poverty, of apostolic spirit, of abdication of any notion of
domination or of tyranny, of religious purity of intention.
It is still singularly applicable. Paul VI meditates on the
De consideratione and is inspired by it. Eugene III could
hardly have applied the program of Saint Bernard, and his
reign was a prelude to the apogee of temporal power under
Innocent III at the end of the same century. Is it not
possible that Paul VI could be the pope that the abbot of
Clairvaux dreamed about.[31]

PLAN

As Dom Jean Leclercq has well demonstrated, the plan
of the *De consideratione* is very carefully worked out and
reveals a very sophisticated art of composition.[1] It
might be outlined as follows:

Book One
  Description of the life of the pope and of his
  difficulties (1–5)
  Consideration
    Exhortation to consideration (6–7)
    Effects of consideration (8–10)
      Fortitude
      Prudence
      Justice
      Temperance
    Applications of consideration (11)
      To the general decadence (12)
      To the abuses of lawyers (13)
      To the ambitious (14)

Book Two
  Division (1–6)
  The Pope himself [Te]
    A man (7; 17–18)
      Rational
      Mortal
    His role (8–13; 15–16)
      Before—a Monk
      Now—Pope
    Moral quality (14; 19–23)

Book Three
  Those below the Pope [Sub te]
    The whole world, not as a possession but to be
    administered (1)
    Various categories
      Heretics (2)
      Gentiles (3–4)
      The ambitious (5)
      Appellants (6–12)
      The avaricious (13)

Impatient prelates (14–18)
Disorderly clerics (19–20)

Book Four
  Those around the Pope [Circa te]
    The clergy and people of the City (1–8)
    Collaborators in the Curia (9–16)
    The Papal household (17–22)
    Epilogue (23)

Book Five
  Those above the Pope [Supra te]
    The spirits (1–6)
      Their nature (7)
      Their species (8–12)

    God
      His nature
        Its principle (13–14)
        'that than which nothing is better' (15)
        Simplicity (16)
        Trinity (17–19)
        Christ the Mediator (20–24)
        The End (24–26)
          The punishment of the proud
          The glory of the humble
      How we possess God (27)

NOTES

1.   tiara: the Latin is *in infulis*. *Infulae* are the lappets of the mitre; they were also found on the papal tiara.

2.   The wordplay is not apparent in the English. The Latin reads . . . *plane ut amans. Amens magis videar*. This type of wordplay (*amans/amens*) is a common characteristic of medieval Latin.

3.   Another common figure in the Latin of the middle ages is the piling up of words of the same root such as is done here: *amans, amat, amoris*.

BOOK ONE

1.   In referring to a limb of the body St Bernard uses the Latin *membrum*. Although the word initially suggests a part of the body, to St Bernard's audience it would have additional overtones. In Chapter 34 of the *Rule* St Benedict speaks of the monks of the community as *omnia membra*. *Membrum* also evokes the New Testament image of Christians as members of Christ; see 1 Cor 6:15.

2.   The two wives of Jacob in Genesis 29 were interpreted by St Augustine as signifying the active life (Leah) and the contemplative life (Rachel). Gregory the Great in his *Homilies on Ezekiel* 2:2 (PL 76:954) borrows Augustine's symbolism. Gregory states: 'Leah and Rachel, the two wives of Jacob, signify these two lives, as has been said before me. Leah means "laborious" and Rachel means "sheep" or "the beginning has been seen." The active life is laborious because it fatigues a person with work; the contemplative life,

on the other hand, is uncomplicated in its eagerness only to see the Beginning, that is, he who says, "I am the Beginning who speak to you." (Jn 8:25) Now, blessed Jacob desired Rachel but at night he accepted Leah. This is to indicate that everyone who turns to the Lord desires the contemplative life and seeks the repose of his eternal home. But before this is attained, he must labor and do good in the night of the present life; that is, he must accept Leah. And then he may attain the vision of the Beginning and rest in the embraces of Rachel.' It seems safe to posit Gregory as a source of Bernard's knowledge of this imagery since we know he knew the *Homilies* from a reference to them in section 12 below. Bernard uses this same image in his *Sermons on the Song of Songs;* see Sermon 9:7; 41:5; 46:5; 51:3.

3.   apostasy: The Latin is *aversio* which implies a turning away from God. Its use in the Vulgate denotes an extreme state of sin, as in Ez 9:9 and Jer 2:19.

4.   Compunction is a technical monastic term. St Benedict uses it in his *Rule* in Chapters 20 and 49 where he speaks of *compunctio lacrimarum* and *compunctio cordis.* Its classical definition was formulated by St Gregory the Great in his *Morals on the Book of Job,* PL 291–292 and *Homilies on Ezekiel,* PL 76:1060, 1070–1071. Jean Leclercq says of compunction that it 'becomes pain of the spirit, a suffering resulting simultaneously from two causes: the existence of sin and our tendency toward sin, and the existence of our desire for God and even our very possession of God.' J. Leclercq, *The Love of Learning and the Desire for God* (New York, 1960) 37–38.

5.   The man is St Augustine who based his definition on Job 28:28 in a pre-Vulgate Latin version of the Bible. He discusses the verse in his *Enchiridion,* expanding it to determine that wisdom, or piety, is the worship of God. 'Now the wisdom of man is piety. This you find in the book of holy Job, for there is written that wisdom herself has said to mankind: "Behold piety is wisdom." But if you ask what manner of piety is meant in this place, you will find a clearer expression in the Greek—*theosebeia,* which is the worship of God *(Dei cultus).* Now piety is also expressed in Greek by another word, *eusebeia,* by which is meant good worship, although this noun also is applied especially to the worship of God. But, since the passage would define the nature of man's wisdom, the most

appropriate word is *theosebeia,* which manifestly conveys the meaning "worship of God." ' St Augustine, *Enchiridion,* trans. Bernard M. Peebles, *The Fathers of the Church,* 4, *The Writings of Saint Augustine* (Washington, D.C., 1937), p. 369.

Augustine thus explains the *Vetus Latina* reading, *pietas,* by referring to the LXX reading, *theosebeia,* and he translates both by *cultus Dei.* This does not, however, justify the source reference by Leclercq to a pre-Vulgate Latin Bible, nor by other editors to the LXX. The statement, *pietas est cultus Dei,* results from these comments on Job 28:28; it is not a direct quote from the Bible. St Augustine uses the phrase several times independently of Job 28:28. In the *City of God* 4:23 he says, 'Piety is true worship of the true God *(Pietas est enim verax veri Dei cultus).*'

A contemporary and friend of St Bernard's, William of St Thierry, frequently used this definition of piety. See *Exposition on the Song of Songs,* trans. Columba Hart OSB, CF 6 (Spencer, 1970), 39, p. 31 and n 26; also *The Golden Epistle,* trans. Theodore Berkeley OCSO, CF 12 (Spencer, 1971), 26f, p. 18 and n 63; 278f, p. 100 and n 36.

6.   The Latin is *quae ipsius quoque actionis partes benigna quadam praesumptione suas facit.* The paradoxical phrase *benigna praesumptio* is perhaps best understood against the background of Bernard's *De gradibus humilitatis et superbiae* in which the seventh degree of pride is *praesumptio.* Therefore, the terms *benigna quadam* are used to neutralize the pejorative connotations of *praesumptio* in this context.

7.   Bernard is fond of using compounds of the same verbal root as he does here: *regit affectus, dirigit actus, corrigit excessus.* Throughout the treatise similar instances occur where the thrust of the statement hinges on the changing prepositional prefixes of a common root.

8.   Here St Bernard aligns the notion of 'consideration' with the definition of wisdom found in Cicero, *On Moral Obligation (De officiis),* 2:5 and *The Tusculan Disputation* 4:57. Also see Seneca, *Letter* 14:1:5. It is repeated by St Augustine in *Against the Academicians* 1:6 where he says that wisdom is the knowledge of human and divine affairs *(sapientiam esse rerum humanarum divinarumque scientiam).*

9.   Aristotle, *Rhetoric* 2:12. The phrase, *ne quid nimis,* is also found in the *Rule* of St Benedict, Chapter 64:12.

10.   The linking of the four principal virtues reflects Plato's thought as transmitted to the Middle Ages by Cicero, Augustine, and Ambrose; the latter was the first to refer to them as *virtutes cardinales.* See Ambrose, *Exposition on the Gospel of Luke* 5:62: 'Indeed we know there are four cardinal virtues: temperance, justice, prudence and fortitude.'

11.   The three virtues to which Bernard addresses himself are justice, temperance, and fortitude; prudence is brought into the discussion later in the paragraph. For several sentences Bernard's discussion of these three virtues and the mean is reminiscent of expressions used to talk about the Trinity. There seems to be an implicit analogy built on the terms so that the mean is to the Divine Nature as the three virtues are to the Persons of the Trinity. See also Book 2:6.

12.   The Latin is *cuique tribuit quod suum est.* This definition of justice has been a commonplace in the West from its introduction by Cicero. See *On the Nature of the Gods* 3:38: *justitia quae suum cuique distribuit.* It is frequently made use of by Christian writers including St Augustine in his *City of God* 19:4: 'It is the task of justice to see that each is given what belongs to him *(justitia, cujus munus est sua cuique tribuere).*'

13.   Here again in his phraseology Bernard puts great emphasis on the force of the verbal prefix: *tempora periculosa non instant jam, sed exstant.*

14.   The Latin is *Miror namque quemadmodum religiosae aures tuae audire sustinent. . . .* The adjective, *religiosus,* throughout the Middle Ages, could regularly be used to refer to the monastic state. Since Bernard is stressing Eugene's unique religious sensibility here, his phrasing calls to mind the fact that the pope is still a monk.

15.   Here Bernard uses compounds: *instruunt, adstruunt, des-truunt, obstruunt.* In this single sentence there are six different forms of *struere.*

16.   ' . . . to avoid frustrating and extortionate delays.' The

Latin is somewhat problematic at this point; the text reads *frustratoriasque et venatorias praecidere dilationes.* Luddy probably captures the sense when he translates: 'delays which are designed for the purpose either of defeating justice or of multiplying fees.' — *St. Bernard's Treatise on Consideration,* trans. A Priest of Mount Mellery [Ailbe Luddy] (Dublin, 1921), p. 28.

BOOK TWO

1. The ensuing discussion which extends through paragraph four, treats the failure of the Second Crusade which Pope Eugene called in December 1145 and which he authorized St Bernard to preach in 1146. Although Louis VII of France was previously committed to the crusade, it was Bernard's inspired preaching at Vezelay in March of 1146 and his subsequent mission to Germany which made the crusade a reality. The Second Crusade came to be closely associated with him. Its failure was not only a blow to the defenses of the Holy Land but also a personal loss to him. This passage is his only extensive comment on that loss. See Virginia Berry, 'The Second Crusade,' in K. M. Setton and M. W. Baldwin, *A History of the Crusades* 1 (1969) pp. 463-512. For Bernard's role, see E. Willems, 'Cîteaux et la second croisade,' in *Revue d'histoire ecclesiastique* 49 (1954) 116-151.

2. Bernard is fond of this kind of wordplay: *reprehendere/ comprehendere.*

3. Here Bernard achieves a chiastic structure with variety (*necesse non est/in necessitate*) and similarity (*scimus/nescimus*) in the balanced clause: *quod scimus cum necesse non est, in necessitate nescimus.*

4. Self-knowledge is the necessary first step in Bernard's mystical theology. Knowledge of self brings personal shame, but at the same time allows awareness of one's creation in God's image. From this double realization come humility and faith, the twin elements which begin all knowledge in Bernard. See Bernard, *De diversis, Sermo* 12:2 (PL 183:571) and Etienne Gilson, *The Mystical Theology of Saint Bernard* (New York, 1940), pp. 70ff.

5. Here, as in Book 1:11, Bernard uses Trinitarian terminology

or imagery to express ideas which are analogous to certain Trinitarian concepts. Bernard sets up the terms of the analogy thus: 'Your word is your consideration. . . .' William of St Thierry discusses the Trinitarian side of this analogy in his *Enigma of Faith;* see Par. 68 of the *Enigma* in CF 9 where William stresses that the Word proceeds from the Father but does not depart from him.

6.   The Latin is *sollicitudo* which offers connotations of care, responsibility or stewardship. It was a term of art for describing the duty of episcopal office. See J. Rivière, ' "In partem sollicitudinis" . . . évolution d'une formule pontificale.' *Revue des sciences religieuses* 5 (1925) 210–231.

7.   In the Latin there is a wordplay on two uses of *opus. Opus* means 'work' but in the idiom *opus est* it means 'there is a need for.'

8.   The Latin is *tabulae testatoris.* This is a variant of the more usual tabulae or *tabulae testamenti* designating a written testament or will. See Adolf Berger. *Encyclopedic Dictionary of Roman Law* (Philadelphia, 1953), p. 733.

9.   Bernard's thought here may well be formed in conscious opposition to the position advanced by Arnold of Brescia. In the 1140s Arnold was agitating in Rome against the papacy on the grounds that all wealth and all temporal power were forbidden the Church by the example of the Apostles. Bernard explicitly modifies that contention here. See G. W. Greenaway, *Arnold of Brescia* (1931), pp. 111–118.

10.   2 Cor 11:28; Cf. note 6 on *sollicitudo.*

11.   The expression 'careful responsibility and responsible care' is an example of the figure of speech called antimetabole.

12.   Here Bernard engages in wordplay based on the similarity of sound between two distantly related words, *puta* and *putationis: puta tempus putationis adesse. . . .* Compare Song 2:12.

13.   Cf. *Rule of St Benedict* 4:62: 'Not to wish to be called holy before one is holy, but first to be holy, that one may more truly be called so.' Bernard uses *summus;* St Benedict uses *sanctus.*

14. Bernard alludes to Prov 9:10 which says, 'The knowledge of the saints is prudence.'

15. Bernard must have in mind Mt 16:19; 1 Cor 5:5; 1 Tim 1:20.

16. The Latin is *perizomata,* which occurs in Gen 3:7 where Adam and Eve become aware of their nakedness and make clothes to cover themselves.

17. The Latin here is more succinct: *nude nudum consideres. . . .*

BOOK THREE

1. Bernard's use of 'mighty wind' in this context is reminiscent of Acts 2:2 where the coming of the Spirit is described as the rush of a mighty wind. By this allusion Bernard explains what he means by the 'powerful arms of God.' The gifts of the Spirit are the weapons of the Apostles.

2. The Latin is *tu curam illius habe* which is found in Lk 10:35 as *Curam illius habe.* These are the words of the Good Samaritan to the innkeeper. By such a use of Biblical language Bernard forges a statement replete with reminiscences which are essential to fill out the complete meaning of what he is saying. Eugene must emulate the compassion of the Good Samaritan in his duties as Pontiff.

3. In this sentence Bernard uses nine different words built on the verb *vertere,* 'to turn.'

4. Rom 10:14. The Latin for this sentence is highly alliterative: *Cui credera casu contigit?*

5. Ps 17:46. Tension over matters of politics and ritual between the Latin and Greek churches had existed even before the dramatic confrontation of 1054. Dogmatic questions were then raised and lingered between the two churches as a result of disputes over unleavened bread and the Photian teaching on the procession of the Holy Spirit. See H. Jedin and J. Dolan, *Handbook of Church History, 4, From the High Middle Ages to the Eve of the Reformation,* pp. 113–119, for a summary and introductory bibliography.

6.   By 1150 the Catharist heresy was well established in the West. The Council of Rheims associated it especially with Gascony and Provence. Cf. Mansi, *Concil.*, 21, 742.

7.   The papacy had attempted to deal with the Cathars by legislative missions. St Bernard himself preached against them in the south in 1146. All early attempts to win them back, however, failed. In his sermons on the Song of Songs, Bernard attributes the failure to the peculiar resistance of this group of heretics to argument from reason or authority and to their success in bribing the clergy, including bishops. Cf. Bernard, *Sermons on the Song of Songs,* 66:14.

8.   Compare this statement in C. H. Haskins, *The Renaissance of the Twelfth Century* (Cleveland, 1957), p. 216: '. . . canon law was stigmatized as a lucrative profession for which men deserted the higher but less remunerative subject of theology.'

9.   See Book 4 where Bernard discusses the things 'around' Eugene.

10.   The bishop in question is Hugh of Mâcon who died on December 10, 1151.

11.   The judges delegate to whom St Bernard refers here were relatively new in 1150. Bishops ordinary, they were appointed to investigate and decide cases locally which had been appealed to the Curia. The advantage of the system was thought to be capacity of the judge delegate to hear all witnesses to the case and to make a decision on the basis of familiarity with the local scene. For the careers of two judges delegate, see Adrian Morey, *Bartholomew of Exeter, Bishop and Canonist: A Study in the Twelfth Century* (Cambridge, 1953) 72–134, and Avrom Saltman, *Theobald, Archbishop of Canterbury* (London, 1956).

12.   Prov 31:21. This section of Proverbs is a description of the virtuous woman asked about in Prov 31:10, 'Who can find a virtuous woman?'

13.   Is 62:5. Bernard interpolates 'your soul' into the Biblical phrase.

14. See Book 1:11 where Bernard speaks of justice.

15. For the Angelic Orders see Gustav Davidson, *A Dictionary of Angels* (New York, 1967) 336–38. Davidson includes several patristic authors and their lists of angels. Bernard may have been familiar with all of them: St Ambrose, St Jerome, St Gregory, Pseudo-Dionysius. It is the nine orders of angels found in Pseudo-Dionysius' *Celestial Hierarchy* which St Thomas Aquinas adopted and which is the traditional order in the Church: Seraphim, Cherubim, Thrones, Dominations, Virtues, Powers, Principalities, Archangels, and Angels. See Book 5:7 where Bernard enumerates the nine choirs of Angels; also *Sermons on the Song of Songs* 19:2–6, CF 4:141–4; 27:5, CF 7:107.

16. Bernard's imagery is borrowed from Song 7:12, 'Let us go out early to the vineyards and see whether the vineyard has bloomed, whether the flowers have borne fruit. . . .' Eugene would not have missed the implicit allusion to the dangers threatening the vineyard which are mentioned in Song 2:15.

17. The Council was held in March of 1148. See Mansi, *Concil.* 21, 716.

18. Bernard uses an ironic play on words here. Speaking of the luxury (*luxus*) of clerical dress, he says, 'we have mourned,' using a form of the verb *lugeo* (*luximus*).

19. This sentence provides internal evidence for dating Book 3 of the treatise in 1152. The decree spoken of was issued at the Council of Rheims in 1148.

20. The English 'multicolored garments . . . disgrace . . .' does not bring across Bernard's play on words in the Latin: *pellicula discolor . . . decolorat . . . .*

BOOK FOUR

1. The Latin for 'household' is *domestica ecclesia.* Here *ecclesia* means 'assembly' or 'gathering.'

2. Revolt against papal government had broken out in Rome in the pontificate of Lucius II (1144–45). Lucius himself was killed

while leading an attack on the Capitol on February 15, 1145, and Eugene III was elected to succeed him. Eugene, however, was unable to re-enter the city and forced to take exile in central Italy, until December 1145. He enjoyed a brief sojourn in the city in 1146 with the military support of Tivoli and Campanian allies, but was soon exiled again. In 1149 Eugene himself collected an army and apparently led it in an assault on Rome, winning part of the city.

3.   The Latin here is carefully constructed for sound: *non tectus auro, non vectus equo albo.*

4.   This is the only allusion in Bernard's work which could be taken as a comment on the forged Donation of Constantine. Edouard Jordan, however, has dismissed the suggestion that this was Bernard's intention here. Cf. Edouard Jordan, 'Dante et saint Bernard,' *Bulletin du Jubilé* (ed. Comité Française Catholique pour la célébration du sixième centenaire de la mort de Dante Alighieri [Paris, 1921] 267–330).

5.   This passage has been of central importance to historians studying St Bernard's ecclesiology. For a discussion of the scholarship on this point, see E. Kennan, 'The *de Consideratione* of St Bernard of Clairvaux and the Papacy in the mid-twelfth century: A Review of Scholarship,' *Traditio* 23 (1967) 73–115.

6.   Bernard does not develop the theory of the two swords further in the *De Consideratione*. He does, however, discuss it in a letter to Eugene on the failure of the Second Crusade, written in 1150: 'Ex serendus est nunc uterque gladius in passione Domini, Christo denuo patiente, ubi et altera vice passus est. Per quam autem nisi per vos? Petri uterque est: alter suo nutu, alter sua manu, quoties necesse est evaginandus. Et quidem de quo minus videbatur, de ipso ad Petrum dictum est: "Converte gladium tuum in vaginam." Ergo suus erat et ille; sed non sua manu utique educendus." ' Bernard, Ep 256 (PL 182.463–64). 'Now, in the passion of the Lord both swords must be drawn, since Christ is suffering again where he suffered on another occasion. By whom if not by you? Both are Peter's; the one must be drawn at his nod, the other by his hand, as often as is necessary. And, about the one which seemed less his, Peter was told concerning that one, "Put your sword in its sheath." Therefore, even that one was his, but it was certainly not to be drawn by his hand.'

7.   This is an example of Bernard's use of the juxtaposition of two verbs from the same root for the sake of a contrast whose meaning is carried by the prefixes: *defecisse* and *profecisse.*

8.   The image of the Church as a widow is a commonplace among early Christian writers. For example, see Augustine, *Enarrationes in Ps.* 131:23.

9.   Martin Cibo, Cistercian Cardinal Priest of St Stefano in Coelio Monte, formerly a monk of Clairvaux, died 1144.

10.   Geoffrey de Lèves, Bishop of Chartres, 1116–1149.

11.   These ministers are deacons, as is made clear below.

12.   Deacon, or *diaconus,* is from the Greek *diakonos* meaning 'servant.'

13.   The Latin here is *providere his qui in sinu tuo et in gremio tuo sunt.*

14.   Mk 12:42. The Latin for the latter part of this sentence is *de minutis et quadrantibus exigentium rationem.*

15.   2 Kings 5:20-27. Gehazi was a servant of Elisha who used his position to obtain fraudulently money and fine clothes from Naaman, the commander of the army of the king of Syria. Elisha cured Naaman's leprosy but would accept no reward from him. Gehazi connived behind Elisha's back to obtain this reward for himself in Elisha's name. Elisha's judgment on Gehazi was that he be stricken with Naaman's leprosy.

16.   The Latin for 'mistress' is *domina.*

BOOK FIVE

1.   Cf. Etienne Gilson, *The Mystical Theology of Saint Bernard,* (New York, London: Sheed and Ward, 1940, 1953) 19-37.

2.   Different patristic and medieval authors give different enumerations and orders for the ranks of the angels. See Gustav

Davidson, *A Dictionary of Angels* (New York, 1967) p. 336.
Bernard's list is that of Gregory the Great in Homily Thirty-four of
the *Forty Homilies on the Gospels.* See PL 76:1249. Bernard treats
of the angels somewhat more fully in his *Nineteenth Sermon on the
Song of Songs,* CF 4:140–144.

3.　Lk 1:26. In his discussion on the angels in this section
Bernard seems to have drawn on Gregory the Great's Homily
Thirty-four, which is cited above. Compare this sentence and one
similar to it in Gregory, PL 76:1250D.

4.　Lk 21:26. The Latin is *Nam virtutes caelorum movebuntur.*
This is usually translated, 'For the powers of heaven will be moved.'
However, Bernard's context here requires a different rendering of
the Latin, such as is given.

5.　Jn 5:35. Also, compare Gregory, Homily Thirty-four,
PL 76:1252B: *Seraphim namque ardentes vel incendentes vocantur.*

6.　Another example of this kind of open admission of ignorance as to the exact meaning of a Biblical expression occurs in
William of St Thierry's *Enigma of Faith,* Par. 39: 'in the next life he
will be thrown into the exterior darkness (whatever that is) which is
read about in the Gospel.'

7.　Ps 26:4. Bernard follows the earlier Latin text which has
voluntatem (will) in place of *voluptatem* (beauty), the now
commonly accepted reading.

8.　Rom 12:2. Why Bernard upsets the balance of his sentence
adding a fourth element in the second part (...good...acceptable...
perfect...: good...pleasing...acceptable...perfect) is clear in the Latin:
*...bona, et beneplacens, et perfecta? Bona...placens...beneplacens
...perfecta....*

9.　Cf. St Anselm, *Proslogium,* 2; tr. S. N. Deane, St. Anselm
(La Salle, IL: Open Court, 1934), p. 8.

10.　Compare William of St Thierry in his *Enigma of Faith,*
Pars. 65 and 76, where the author discusses *triplicitas* (tripleness or
three-foldness) as a term not applicable to the reality of the Trinity.
Bernard is here rejecting the condemned teaching of Gilbert of

Poitiers; Mansi, *Concil.* 21:711.

11. Bernard's language is carefully chosen here to say all that he wants to say. His God is universal; his God is the God of the Catholic Church. The Latin is *Meus Deus ipse catholice est.*

12. Here, *forma* is used with the meaning of the exterior appearance resulting from the placement of quantitative parts. Form, in this sense, is not applicable to God.

13. *ut istis visum est:* Bernard seems to be referring here to Gilbert of Poitiers and his followers. See SC 80:6-9, *S. Bernardi opera,* edd. Leclercq et al., 2:281ff and the notes there. In the next paragraph (17—see note 14 below) Bernard quotes the text of Boethius which he commends in SC 80:8 and which was the subject of Gilbert's erroneous commentary.

14. Bernard's Latin here is *unissimus est!*

15. Bernard's formulation here is undoubtedly influenced by the 'Athanasian' Creed which he chanted each Sunday at the office of Prime. See note 16 below.

16. Bernard's language here is that of Section 37 of the 'Athanasian' Symbol. See H. Denzinger, *Enchiridion Symbolorum* (Rome, 1967) p. 42. The Symbol states, 'Just as the rational soul and the flesh are one man, so God and man are one Christ.'

17. Here also Bernard's expression is that of the 'Athanasian' Symbol.

APPENDICES

The Recipient

1. Bernard of Clairvaux, Ep 237:1, PL 182:426B; tr. James, *Letter* 315, p. 385.

2. 'Bibliographie sur Eugène III' in *Bibliotheca Sanctorum* 5:200.

3.   Bernard of Clairvaux, Ep 237:3, PL 182:427AB; tr. James, *Letter* 315, p. 386.

4.   Idem, Ep 238, PL 182:427–431; tr. James, *Letter* 205, pp. 277–280.

5.   Ibid., no. 6, 430B, tr. p. 279.

6.   Ibid., no. 7, 430D.

Date of Composition

1.   PL 189:409.

2.   Csi 2:1–4.

3.   Csi 3:20.

4.   *Vita prima,* 5:1, PL 185:351.

5.   A. H. Bredero, 'Un brouillon du XIIe siècle: l'autographe de Geoffrey d'Auxerre,' *Scriptorium* 13 (1959) 33–58.

Manuscripts

1.   Concerning the text of the *De consideratione* and its manuscripts see *S. Bernardi opera,* vol. 3: *Tractatus et opuscula,* ed. J. Leclercq and H. M. Rochais (Rome: Editiones Cistercienses, 1963) 381–392.

Sources

1.   Arnaud de Bonneval, *Vita prima,* 2:51, PL 185:298.

2.   *De doctrina christiana,* 1:22: 'Cum ergo quatuor sint diligenda, unum quod supra nos est, alterum quod nos sumus, tertium quod iuxta nos est, quartium quod infra nos est, de secundo et quarto nulla praecepta danda erant.' PL 34:27. Cf. F. Ohly, 'Goethe Erfurchten ein ordo caritatis,' *Euphorion* 55 (1961) 115–145.

3.   *De clericorum institutione,* 3:4, PL 107:381B.

4. *De fide, spe et charitate*, 3:5, PL 120:1467B.

5. Jean Leclercq, 'L'Art de la composition dans les traités de s. Bernard,' *Recueil d'études sur saint Bernard*, vol. 3 (Rome: Edizioni de Storia e Letteratura, 1969) 131–132.

6. *Expositio regulae ab Hildemaro tradita*, ed. Mittermuller (Ratisbonne, 1880) p. 70.

7. 'Miminisse debet quod est. Quid est, quia homo est; quod est, quia praelatus est.' Ibid., p. 117.

8. Ibid., pp. 168–169. See Jean Leclercq, *Études sur saint Bernard et le teste de ses écrits*. Analecta SOC 9 (1953) p. 147. Hildemar seems to have inspired a first draft of the *De consideratione:* 'Solioquium ipsius (Domni Bernardi abbatis) de consideratione quadripertita propriae conditionis.' Ibid., p. 148.

9. Csi 5:16, p. 481: *De Trinitate* 2, ed. R. Peiper (1871) p. 153.

10. *De vita s. Adalhardi*, PL 120:1517A.

11. H. Hürten, 'Gregor der Grosse und der mitteralterliche Episkopat,' *Zeitschrift für Kirchengeschichte* 76 (1965) 16–41.

12. A. de Vogüé, 'La règle de s. Benoît et la vie contemplative,' *Collectanea OCR* 27 (1965) 92, n. 6.

13. St. Gregory, *Regulae pastoralis liber*, PL 77:17B; Csi 1:1–4, pp. 394–397.

14. Csi 3:4, p. 433; 1:12, p. 407.

15. E. Bertola, *San Bernardo e la teologia speculativa* (Padua, 1959) 53–54.

16. *Rhetorica* 2:12. *Ne quid nimis*, I, 8, 9.

17. M. Déchanet, *Saint Bernard Théologien*, pp. 61–77. 'Aux sources de la pensée philosophique de s. Bernard.'

18. Csi 5:32, p. 493.

19. Horace, *Satires* I, 1:92.

20. Csi 4:2, p. 450.

21. See B. Jacquelin, *Papauté et épiscopat selon saint Bernard de Clairvaux* (Saint-Lô, 1963) p. 61, and J. Leclercq, 'Marie reine dans les sermones marials de saint Bernard,' *Collectanea OCR* 26 (1964) 265–276.

Influence

1. MGH II, 301:16. H. Weisweiler, 'Drei unveröffentliche Briefe aus dem christologischen Streit Gerhochs von Reichersberg,' *Scholastik* 13 (1938) 44–45; D. van den Eynde, *L'Oeuvre littéraire de Gerhoch de Reichersberg* (Rome, 1957) pp. 213, 225–230; P. Classen, *Gerhoch von Reichersberg. Eine Biographie* (Weisbaden, 1960) 363–364.

2. *Policraticus* 4:7, 5:7, 16, 7:2, 8:23.

3. Csi 4:13.

4. PL 217:555.

5. Csi 2:16.

6. PL 217:657.

7. Csi 2:9–13.

8. Ibid. 4:23.

9. PL 217:638.

10. Csi 2:16.

11. Ibid. 4:7. J. Rivière, *Le problème de l'Eglise et de l'Etat au temps de Philippe le Bel* (Paris–Louvain, 1916) 405–424. Cardinal Lemoine (Corpus Juris [Lyon, 1617], t. III, III, can. 208) referred to the *De consideratione* to gloss the Bull *Unam Sanctam*.

12. 'E quando non basti cio ai cavillatori, leggemo Ricardo di

San Vittore nel libro sulla contemplazione, leggemo Bernardo nel libro sulla considerazione.' Ep. 13:2.

13. E. Parodi, 'La data della composizione e le idee politiche dell'Inferno e del Purgatorio,' *Poesie e Storia nella Divina Commedia* (Naples, 1921) p. 364ff.

14. *Monarchia*, III, 3, 8, 9, and 15.

15. Csi 1:7, 4:7.

16. Csi 5:32.

17. P. Lehmann, 'Konstanz und Basel als Büchermarkte während der Grossen Kirchenversammlunger,' *Erforschung des Mittelalters* (Leipzig, 1914) 273–277.

18. *Camaldoli* 7 (1953) p. 50.

19. Leclercq, *Etudes*, p. 38.

20. M. Bertola, *I due primi registri di prestito della Biblioteca Apostolica Vaticana* (Vat. lat. 3964–3966), (Vatican City, 1942) pp. 5, 15; 82, 19; 119, 13.

21. Ms. Vat. Lat. 658; it is described by Dom Leclercq in *Etudes*, p. 45.

22. Paul de Vooght, 'Du *De consideratione* de saint Bernard au *De potestate papae* de Wiclif,' *Irenikon* 26 (1935) 114–132.

23. *Epistola*, ed. Allen (1922) 1:1202.

24. *La Consideratione*, tr. Senlis (Paris, 1943).

25. 'Memoriale P. Consalvi,' *Monumenta Ignatii*, IV, I, p. 199 and 316.

26. A. Deroo, *Saint Charles Borromée* (Paris, 1963) p. 289.

27. Preface to the edition of Gérard Vosius (1594) dedicated to Clement VIII (1536–1605).

28. Csi 2:23 in *Provinciale XVIII.*

29. Csi 2:15. See A. G. Martimort, *Le Gallicanisme de Bossuet* (Paris, 1953) p. 488.

30. (Paris, 1964) p. 459.

31. R. Rouquette, 'Paul VI héritier de Jean XXIII,' *Etudes* 310 (1963) 259.

Plan

1. Jean Leclercq, 'L'Art de la composition . . . ,' pp. 117–130.

SELECTED BIBLIOGRAPHY

The bibliography of studies on Saint Bernard is so extensive that three successive volumes have been required to keep it up to date. These should be consulted by anyone interested in pursuing Bernard studies.

L. Janauschek. *Bibliographia Bernardina.* Vienna, 1891, rpt. Georg Olms, Hildesheim, n.d.

Jean de la Croix Bouton. *Bibliographie Bernardine 1891-1957.* Commission d'histoire de l'ordre de Cîteaux, No. v. Paris: P. Lethielleux, 1958.

Eugène Manning. *Bibliographie Bernardine (1957-1970). Documentation Cistercienne* 6 (1972).

The eighth centenary of the death of Bernard, 1953, brought forth several congresses and publications concerning the saint. Among these are:

Bernhard von Clairvaux: Mönch und Mystiker. Internationaler Bernhardkongress, Mainz 1953. Veröffentlichungen des Instituts für europäische Geschichte Mainz, 6, Wiesbaden: Franz Steiner Verlag, 1955.

Mélanges St. Bernard: 24e Congrès de l'Association bourguignonne de sociétés savantes. Dijon, 1954.

Saint Bernard Théologien. Actes du Congrès de Dijon. Analecta SOC 9 (1953).

Good general studies on Saint Bernard and his role in the twelfth-century Church include:

Louis Bouyer. *The Cistercian Heritage.* Tr. Elizabeth Livingstone. London: Mowbray, 1958.

Henri Daniel-Rops. *Bernard of Clairvaux.* Tr. Elizabeth Abbott. New York: Hawthorne, 1964.

Odo J. Egres. *Saint Bernard, his life and teaching.* Frosinone: Casamari Abbey, 1961.

Etienne Gilson. *The Mystical Theology of Saint Bernard.* Tr. A.H.C. Downes. New York: Sheed and Ward, 1940, 1955.

Charles Homer Haskins. *The Renaissance of the Twelfth Century.* Cambridge, Mass.: Harvard University Press, 1927; Cleveland: Meridian, 1957.

Bruno Scott James. *St Bernard of Clairvaux: An Essay in Biography.* London, 1957.

Elizabeth T. Kennan. 'The *De Consideratione* of St Bernard of Clairvaux and the Papacy in the mid-twelfth century: A Review of Scholarship,' *Traditio* 23 (1967) 73–115.

David Knowles. 'Saint Bernard of Clairvaux, 1090–1153.' *Dublin Review* 227 (1953) 104–121.

Jean Leclercq. *The Love of Learning and the Desire for God.* New York: Fordham University Press, 1960, 1974.

———. *Recueil d'études sur saint Bernard.* 3 vols. Rome: Edizione de Storia et letteratura, 1962, 1966, 1969.

———. *St Bernard et l'esprit cistercien.* Paris: Seuil, 1966. ET to appear as CS 16 (1975).

———. *Saint Bernard mystique.* Bruges, 1948.

Ailbe J. Luddy. *The Life and Teaching of St Bernard.* 2nd ed. Dublin: Gill, 1950.

Denis Meadows. *A Saint and a Half: A New Interpretation of Abelard and St Bernard of Clairvaux.* New York: Devin and Adair, 1963.

Thomas Merton. *The Last of the Fathers: Saint Bernard of Clairvaux and the Encyclical Letter.* Doctor Mellifluus. New York: Harcourt, Brace; London: Hollis and Carter, 1954.

Zoe Oldenbourg. *Saint Bernard presenté par Z. Oldenbourg.* Le Mémorial des siècles: XIIe siècle: les hommes. Paris, Editions Albin Michel, 1970.

Elphegius Vancandad. *Vie de saint Bernard.* Paris, 1894.

Watkin Williams. *Saint Bernard of Clairvaux.* Manchester: University Press, 1935, 1953.

———. *Studies in St Bernard of Clairvaux.* London, 1927.

Editions of the *De consideratione* include:

De consideratione. Utrecht: Nicholaus Ketelaer and Gerardus Leempt, c. 1473.

De consideratione. Augsburg: Anton Sorg, c. 1476/7.

De consideratione. Paris: Pierre Levet, c. 1496.

Beati Bernardi Clareuallensis De consideratione ad Eugenium Papam Tertium libri quinque. . . nouissime emendati. . . . Paris: Reginald Chaudiere, 1515?

. . . De consideratione ad Evgenivm libri V. Eivsdem De praecepto & dispensatione libellus. Antwerp: C. Plantini, 1571.

S. Bernardi Abbatis Claraevallis. De consideratione ad Eugenium papam tertium, libri quinque. . . . Rome: Gulielmi Facciotti, 1594.

. . . De consideratione ad Eugenium papam libri v. Paris: apud Mequignon juniorem, 1828.

S. Bernardi claraevallensis abbatis De consideratione, libri V. Ad Eugenium III . . . .. Landihuti: Libraria I. Thomanni, 1845.

De consideratione libri V. Berlin: C. Wiegandt, 1850.

De consideratione libri V. ad Eugenium III et tractatus de Mori-bus et Officio Episcoporum. . . . Innsbruck: Libraria Aca-demica Wagneriana, 1868.

De consideratione ad Eugenium papam libri V. . . . Paris: A. Roger et F. Chernoviz, 1868.

. . . *De consideratione, libri V ad Eugenium III.* . . . London: D. Nutt; Paris: P. Lethielleux, 1885.

The most easily accessible are:

J.-P. Migne. *Patrologiae cursus completus, series latina* (Paris, 1844–64), vol. 182: 727–808.

Jean Leclercq and Henri Rochais, edd. *Sancti Bernardi Opera, III.* Rome: Editiones Cistercienses, 1957. Pp. 379–494.

Translations into modern languages include:

Saint Bernard On consideration. Tr. George Lewis. Oxford: Clarendon Press, 1908.

St. Bernard's Treatise on consideration, translated from the ori-ginal Latin by a priest of Mount Melleray. Dublin: Brown and Nolan, 1921.

Traité de S. Bernard, de la consideration au pape Eugene. . . Tr. par Gabriel. Paris: Bresche, 1672.

Traité de la consideration. Tr. J.A.C. Choix d'ouvrages mystiques. Paris, 1840.

Oeuvres complètes de saint Bernard. Tr. Charpentier. Paris: L. Vives, 1865. Vol. 2, pp. 125–235.

Oeuvres de saint Bernard. Tr. Armand Ravelet. Bar-le-duc: L. Guerin, 1870. Pp. 119–191.

Conseils au Pape. Tr. Pierre Dalloz. Paris: Editions de Minuit, 1945. (Selections).

La considération. Tr. Pierre Dalloz. Grenoble: Didier & Richard, 1945.

Papst und papstthum nach der Zeichnung des h. Bernhard von Clairvaux. Tr. Jos. Hub. Reinkens. Münster: Brunn, 1870.

ANALYTIC INDEX

Roman numerals refer to books; arabic numerals to paragraphs
(Roman numerals within books are not included in this index)

Adversity
I:8; II:21; IV:12, 19.
Affliction
I:3,4; III:6,14
Ambition
I:5,13; III:5,18
Angels
I:7; III:18; V:5,7,10,12,18
Orders of angels V:7 ff.
Apostasy
I:2
Apostle(s)
I:4,7,; II:7,9,11-13,15; III:2,17;
VI:6,7
See also, The Apostle
Apostolic Office
I:5; II:11
Apostolic right
II:10
Appeal (legal)
III:7-12
Arrogance
III:16,20; IV:2
Austerity
IV:22
Authority
I:5,14; II:14; IV:19; V:5
Avarice
I:5; II:23; III:13,14
See also Greed

Benefice
III:8,19,20
Bishop(s)
I:5,7; II:15-17; III:8,11,13,16,18-
20; IV:1,13, 19-21,23

Blasphemy
II:1,22; V:16
Body of Christ
III:5,17

Charity
Preface; I:5; V:12,19,29,31
See also Love
Comprehension
V:27,30
Compunction
I:3; IV:20
Conscience
I:5,12; II:4,14; III:4,14; IV:5,14,
20; V:25
Consideration
I:6,8,9-11,14; II:4-8,12-13,17-19,
20-23; III:2,9,13,14,19; IV:1,
17,18; V:1-5,9,19
Consubstantiality
I:19
Contemplation
II:5; V:3,4,32
Contempt
I:4; II:10,12; IV:22
Courts (law)
I:13
Cross of Christ
II:12
Curia, The Roman
III:8,13; IV:9,10,15,17

Damnation
III:10
Death
III:1,16; IV:6; V:21-22, 25-26

217

Depravity
  I:1; III:7
Discipline
  II:21; III:19; IV:12,21
Discretion
  II:20
Dispensation
  III:18
Divine Office
  IV:22
Divinity
  I:3; V:15-17, 21-22

Ecstasy
  V:3,32
Elect, the
  V:9
Election (episcopal)
  II:9; III:11
Essence
  I:8; II:17; V:13,16-17,19-20,22
Exemption(s)
  III:16
Exile
  II:19; V:1
Experience
  I:1; IV:1,25; V:24,26,20

Faith
  II:3,13; III:2-4,14; IV:12,15,19,
    23: V:5-7,18,21
Fasting
  I:10; II:1
Flatterers
  II:22; IV:19
Flattery
  Preface; IV:4,10
Fool(s)
  Preface; I:4,6; II:11
Foolish
  II:14; III:2; IV:23
Fortitude
  I:8,9,11; V:25
Friend(s)
  II:8; IV:13
Frivolity
  II:21,22; IV:22
Generosity
  I:6
Grace
  I:3; V:3,5
Greed

Preface; III:5
  See also Avarice
Guilt
  II:18

Heretics
  III:3
Heresy
  III:4 (false doctrine III:19)
Humanity
  I:3; II:17; IV:23
  See also Man
Humility
  II:4,13; IV:10; V:32

Idleness
  II:9,22
Imagination
  V:2

Judgment
  I:6,7,9,11,13;   II:1-2,4,8,20,23;
    III:12,15; IV:12,22; V:32
Justice
  I:8,10-11,13; II:2,13; III:7,9-10,
    14,17; IV:9,12; V:26

Knowledge
  I:8; II:14; V:1,8,10-11,24,27
Labor
  I:1,5; II:10-12,18; III:12; IV:1-3,
    12
Law(s)
  I:5; III:15,19-20; IV:12,23
Lawyers
  I:13
Leisure
  I:4,11-12,14; II:10,22; III:5; IV:
    1-2,12; V:32
Liberty
  III:16; V:2,9
Love
  Preface; III:17; IV:4,11,23: V:9-
    13,30,31
  See also Charity
Luxury
  II:10; III:20

Man
  I:6; II:2,7,13-14,17-18; III:2: V:
    12,20-22 *et passim*

rational animal II:7
Marriage(s)
 III:8,11 (conjugal union V:18)
Meditation
 I:5; II:13
 to meditate III:15; V:32
Memory
 V:26,32
Mind
 I:8,10; II:5,18; V:7
Ministry
 II:10,13-14; III:17; V:9
Moderation
 I:9,10; II:10; III:13; IV:21-22
 See also Temperance
Monk(s)
 III:16
Mortality
 II:7

Nature
 II:17-18; III:15; V:5

Obedience
 IV:22
Opinion
 V:5-7

Patience
 I:4; IV:12; V:32
Peace
 I:1; II:1; IV:2,8,12; V:7,9,11
Perfection
 II:8,14-15; III:14
Philosopher(s)
 II:7; V:14
Philosophy
 I:12; III:15; V:3
Pilgrimage
 V:2
Poor, the
 Preface; I:6,13; II:18; III:13; IV:
 5,12,23
 See also Poverty
Poverty
 III:16
Power
 III:14-15,17; V:14,29
 divine power IV:2; V:23
Prayer
 I:14: IV:12,23; V:5
Preaching

III:4,20; IV:6,23
Predestination
 V:21
Property (material)
 I:7; III:16; IV:12,19
Prudence
 I:8-9,11; II:22; IV:18-19
Punishment
 II:13; III:6,19,20; V:25

Quaternity
 V:15,27

Rationality
 II:7
 See also Reason
Reading
 V:7
Reason
 I:14; III:15; IV:16; V:5,13,18,
 26
 See also Rationality
Redemption
 II:18; III:1
Reputation
 III:14; IV:12
Responsibility
 II:8-10,12
Rich, the
 Preface; I:6; III:13; IV:12
 See also Wealth
Righteousness
 III:3; V:25

Sacraments
 III:10; IV:2
Sacrilege
 I:5; II:1,22; III:8
Salvation
 I:3; II:6-7; IV:5; V:3,9,12,20,23
Self-knowledge (discussion of)
 II:14,19
Self-seekers
 IV:9
Sense(s), bodily
 V:1,4,26
Servant(s)
 I:7; II:11,13; III:2; IV:6,20-22
 of Christ II:11
Servitude
 I:4-5; V:23
Shepherd

I:5; II:15; IV:3,6,23
Simony
   I:5
Simplicity
   I:13; V:16,27
Sin
   I:4,7; II:1,13; III:19-20; IV:21;
      V:23
Solitude
   I:1
Soul(s)
   I:2,5; III:17; IV:3,20; V:9,12,
      21-23,26
Steward
   II:12; III:1,2
Stewardship
   III:1
Substance
   V:12,14,17-18,28

Teacher
   Preface; II:8-9; III:2,17; VI:23;
      V:27
Temperance
   I:9-11
   See also Moderation
Tranquility
   V:10-11
Trinity
   V:18-20,27
Two Swords
   IV:7

Understanding
   I:4; II:20; IV:23; V:5-8,11,27-28
Unity
   II:15; IV:12; V:18-22,27,29

Vengeance
   I:3; II:13
Vicar of Christ
   II:16; IV:23
Vice(s)
   I:11; II:20,23; III:13-14
Virtue(s)
   I:4,9-11; II:13-14, 19-21; V:2,
      11,32
   Type of angels V:7 ff.

Wealth
   II:10; IV:3; V:3
   See also Rich, the

Will
   I:10; II:13; V:8,25
   of God V:9
Wisdom
   I:10,12; II:4,6,13,20-21; III:2,4;
      IV:10; V:2,8,24,29,31

Zeal
   I:14; II:20; III:9,13; IV:12; V:
      10,24

INDEX OF PROPER NAMES

Aaron
   II:15
Abel
   II:15
Abraham
   I:6; IV:2,14; V:9
Achab
   III:15
Adam
   V:23
Alexander
   II:14
Antiochus
   II:14
Apostle, The (St Paul)
   I:6-7,9; II:10-12,15,19; III:2,6,
      13; V:5,28
   See also Paul
Aquitaine
   IV:14
Augustine (of Canterbury)
   III:4
Augustus
   II:14
Auxerre
   III:11

Benjamin
   II:3
Boethius
   V:17

Christ
   I:5,14; II:4,11,14,15; III:1,4,12;
      IV:12,21,24; V:19,20-23,28
   See also Savior
Cologne
   III:13

Constantine
IV:6

Dacia
IV:13

Egypt
II:2
Egyptians, the
II:1
Elijah
IV:12
Elisha
IV:12
English, the
III:4
Ephraim
I:1
Ezekiel
I:12

Fathers, the
III:13
Florence
IV:13
French, the
III:11

Gabriel
V:8
Gehazi
IV:22
Gentiles, the
III:2,3
Geoffrey of Chartres
IV:14
Germans, the
III:13
Greeks, the
III:2,4
Gregory the Great
I:12; III:4

Isaac
II:3
Israelites, the
II:2,3
Italians, the
III:5

Jacob, House of
IV:8

James
II:15
Jethro
I:3
Jerusalem
III:18; V:7
Jesse
V:23
Jews
I:4; III:2
John
IV:12
Joseph (of Egypt)
IV:19
Judas
IV:19
Justinian
I:5

Mainz
III:13
Martin (of Tours)
IV:13
Mary, B.V.
V:8,22,23
Melchisedeck
II:15
Moses
II:2,15; III:17; IV:9,12; V:13

Nathan
III:15
Noah
II:15

Paris
III:11
Paul
I:4,5,10; II:11; III:17; IV:2,5,12,
    17,20; V:1,3,8,29
    See also Apostle, the
Peter
II:15,16; III:4; IV:5,6,12
Pharoah
I:3
Philip
III:4
Phineas
IV:12

Rachel
I:1

Rebecca
  II:13
Rheims, Council of
  III:19
Rome
  III:8,11,13
  'The City' IV:1,4
Romans, the
  III:13; IV:2

Samuel

II:15; IV:14
Satan
  II:16
Savior
  II:13; IV:19; V:8
  See also Christ
Solomon
  I:6

Ur of the Chaldees
  IV:8

CPSIA information can be obtained
at www.ICGtesting.com
Printed in the USA
FSHW010627210119
55108FS